Dennis Miller Ranting Again

Books by
Dennis Miller

THE RANTS

Dennis Miller

Ranting Again

MAIN STREET BOOKS

Doubleday

New York   London   Toronto
Sydney   Auckland

MAIN STREET BOOKS

A MAIN STREET BOOK
PUBLISHED BY DOUBLEDAY
a division of Random House, Inc.
1540 Broadway, New York, New York 10036

MAIN STREET BOOKS, DOUBLEDAY, and the portrayal of a
building with a tree are trademarks of Doubleday, a division of
Random House, Inc.

Book design by Terry Karydes

The Library of Congress has cataloged the Doubleday edition as follows:
Miller, Dennis, comedian.
Ranting again / Dennis Miller.
p.   cm.
Continues: Rants. 1996.
I. Miller, Dennis, comedian. Rants.   II. Title.
PN6162.M488   1998   792.7′028′092—dc21
97-44475
CIP

ISBN 0-385-48853-X
First Main Street Books Edition: July 1999
1   3   5   7   9   10   8   6   4   2

For Carolyn (Ali), Holden, and Marlon-Olivier.

You are the loves of my life.

Contents

Contents

Contents

Preface

The Rants originally appeared on my HBO
show *Dennis Miller Live*. I'd like to thank David
Feldman, Eddie Feldman, Mike Gandolfi, Jim Hanna,
Tom Hertz, Leah Krinsky, Rick Overton, Jacob
Weinstein, and David Weiss for their assistance. I'd also
like to thank Bruce Tracy and Eliza Truitt at
Doubleday, Kevin Slattery, and Marc Gurvitz. Also Jeff
Bewkes, Chris Albrecht, and Carolyn Strauss at HBO.
And, most important, I'd like to thank Michael Fuchs
for his unwavering belief in me. Now I don't want to
get off on a rant here, but . . .

Dennis Miller Ranting Again

The Single Life

Now, I don't want to get off on a rant here, but I'm glad my single days are over.

Sure I hear guys talking about personal freedom. How they don't have to answer to anybody and how they're meeting all sorts of new people. But the grim reality is that scientists estimate that the average American male spends a full four days of his single life hearing the phrase "Pull the car over, asshole, I'm walking."

There's so much paranoia and mistrust between the sexes, it makes the war room in *Dr. Strangelove* look like the Jacuzzi at Plato's Retreat.

Sure, everybody loves the show *Friends,* but, come on, that's not singles reality. In the real singles world you live in an apartment the size of Billy Barty's walk-in closet with three roommates who are flakier than a Greek pastry placed on Wally George's shoulder. Roommates who two weeks into the relationship tell you they spent their rent money on a QVC alabaster statuette of Hermann Göring that they are hollowing into a bong. While striving for independence, you begin to realize that you've become a day care center for a bunch of lazy sleep farmers.

So let's just say that *Friends,* while it's a great show, is not exactly a reconnaissance photo of the day-to-day machinations of the solo life. That being said, it's a lot better than the single people I saw on TV growing up. Eb, Jethro, Tony Nelson, and Major Healy. No wonder my single life seemed to go on forever. I was walking around in an Elmer Fudd hat and a rope belt looking for a genie to blow me.

For me, dating was like a casting call for *America's Most Wanted.* I once dated a girl who was so twisted, her personalities formed their own softball league.

My life was emptier than Richard Harris's minibar at the Château Marmont.

I was so desperate when I told my friends: "Hey, there are other fish in the sea," I meant other fish. Folks, what I'm saying is, I fucked saltwater seafood. Wasn't proud of it then. Not proud of it now. As a matter of fact, I proba-bly wouldn't have brought it up if this rant wasn't running a little short.

Dennis Miller

Not that the women who dated me had it easy either. When I eventually did get a date, I got so excited, I looked like Martini when he finally got the boat ride in *Cuckoo's Nest*.

Toward the end of my single life I was frozen with fear about how to even go about meeting my soul mate. I mean, c'mon, singles bars? Do you know how hard it was for me to keep a straight face while some stoner broad told me what she thought Pink Floyd meant on *The Dark Side of the Moon?*

Personal ads? I just don't know if I'd be comfortable trying to communicate with my future spouse the same way the cops contacted the Zodiac Killer in *Dirty Harry*.

And, of course, the newest way for singles to meet each other is through their home computers, on-line. And I don't want to burst your bubble, Spanky-dot-com, but, uh, y'know all those succulent Hawaiian Tropic chicks you think you're trading fantasies with are actually fifty-year-old fat guys who make Abe Vigoda look like Marcus Schenkenberg. Forget computers. Humans need physical contact. I'll take the clap over carpal tunnel syndrome any day.

And, single people, if you still don't get it, I'll translate it for the commitment-impaired. Marriage is a never-ending series of one-night stands.

And I'm on the biggest hot streak of my life. So forget single, wake up and smell the stranger next to you.

Marriage is the last step of personal evolution. It is the opposable thumb of human intimacy. So come out of the ape cage and give Darwin your phone number, dammit!

Of course, that's just my opinion, I could be wrong.

Dennis Miller

Generation X

Now, I don't want to get off on a rant here, but isn't it about time we got off generation X's tattooed back? It's no wonder Xers are angst-ridden and rudderless. They feel America's greatness has passed. They got to the cocktail party twenty minutes too late and all that's left are those little wieners and a half-empty bottle of Zima.

So that's why they're threatened. But why do we find *them* so threatening? I thought we were a little hipper than that. Or at least we were when we were their age.

You must remember that then, as now, it remains the single most important function of a generation to irk the living shit out of the generation immediately preceding it.

Screw the old squares, listen to a faster beat, wear a wider cuff, get a Beavis and Gingrich tattoo, change. Life is about change. More than that, life is like riding the bus, it *requires* change.

The so-called generation X has gotten a bad rap for being whiners. But people in their twenties have always been whiners. People in their twenties *should* be whiners. They are to whining what Pavarotti is to . . . uh . . . uh . . . *Tommy*. Okay, I don't know opera.

The reason you whine is that you've just popped out of the cozy, beer-filled amniotic sac of academia.

You haven't developed the prerequisite thick hide of the cynical, callused bastard yet, and your future seems bleaker than Ingmar Bergman listening to an acoustic set performed by Leonard Cohen.

Add to the angst bouillabaisse the current prospects of a flatlining economy, an environment that's choking to death on its own shit, and a sexual atmosphere that's about as warm, safe, and inviting as a Zagreb bunker. Christ, if I were in my twenties now, I'd be bitching so hard, I'd make Beck sound like Tony Newley.

Additionally, this generation of young adults is being forced to experience every coltish fumble of their coming of age with the media doing a hushed, reverentially breathless play-by-play. It's kinda like if Dr. Frankenstein gave a running commentary of what the monster was doing all day.

What's the result of all that scrutiny? It would appear, mass-marketed nonconformity. *The Real World* holding auditions. Auditions. For the fucking "real world." Everyone's so busy playing to the cameras that nobody's creating anything. That's why they use all of our stuff. The Brady Bunch, platform shoes, Tony Bennett.

They suffer from generational performance anxiety because we baby boomers are constantly pounding our chests about our salad days. To hear us tell it, the late sixties and early seventies were a time where between orgies everybody got together and put on Woodstock. Then, between band breaks, we put a stop to an unjust war and brought a rogue chief executive officer to his knees, all the while smoking the most incredible cheap herb in the history of the dilated planet.

You know, they heard all about the free love of the sixties and seventies. But now it's the nineties, the balloon payment is due, and their generation has to pay the mortgage. Instead of casual sex, they have precautionary sex. Nothing ruins the mood during foreplay more than the recurring image of your sixty-five-year-old homeroom teacher trying to stretch a condom over a cucumber.

So believe me, I understand the origins of their discontent. And I empathize. Having said that, I'll be damned if I know what makes these kids tick.

It appears their personal philosophy places a great deal of value on getting so many body piercings that you begin to look like you fell down a flight of stairs carrying a tackle box.

Body-piercing. A powerful, compelling visual statement that says "Gee . . . in today's competitive job market, what can I do to make myself even *more* unemployable?"

Fashion is an interesting sword when wielded by disaffected youth. Any guy that remembers being a teenager knows that many youthful uprisings take place in pants, so the practicality of wearing them so big you could smuggle a hard-on the size of a beagle is not lost on me.

Well, what else is important to them? As far as stimulants go, both of our generations know the feeling of jonesing for product from Colombia; it's just that their product is coffee.

And by the way, is it asking too much to be able to drink a cup of joe in public without having to listen to some malcontent working out their issues, next to me? It's bad enough that these coffeehouses all seem to have purchased their furniture at the same Dresden fire sale, and when the guy who's been occupying a table for the entire time he's been growing his goatee finally gets up and clears away his journal and his clove cigarettes and his Tibetan worry beads and you can finally sit down, you realize that the table is wobbling because one leg is so much shorter than all the others that the only thing that would balance it is a hardcover copy of Marcel Proust's *Remembrance of Things Past,* and you're finally enjoying your café whatever and your triple-berry chocolate-chip six-grain scone when some chick with a buzz cut wearing cat's-eye sunglasses, an orange-and-avocado-green feathered JoAnne Worley "sock-it-to-me" dress, and combat boots stands up front and starts reading a poem she wrote about the first guy who ever felt her up.

All right, so I just tipped my hand. Maybe I'm not as comfy with these kids as I let on. Maybe it's true. Maybe there is a gap between the baby boomers and the generation Xers that makes the Khyber Pass look like the eye of a needle. How did that happen?

Well, I'll tell you how it happened. It happened because we have become our parents, the caretakers of the status quo, set in our ways, afraid of change, prattling on and on about our Ford Windstars while tapping our feet to Wang Chung in our dentist's waiting room.

Look, sure Xers are *pissed,* and they're just beginning to understand that it's because we owe them and we haven't said a damn word about it. It's like that friend who owes you money but makes you feel like an asshole for bringing it up.

Well, trust me, fellow elders, it's time to brace up and get ready because natural progression dictates that they'll get over their shyness soon and start banging on our doors like a shortchanged Chinese takeout guy. They are our ghosts of Christmas past, and if you listen closely you can hear them rattling their nose chains.

Meet the new boss, same as the old boss, except for the Doc Martens and the purple hair.

Of course, that's just my opinion, I could be wrong.

Animal Rights

Can I be so bold as to advance the radical notion that humans earn rights by living by a commonly accepted set of rules, and all you have to do is go to the zoo and watch the monkeys spend their day whacking off right in front of you to know they just don't play by our rules. All you can do is just stand there, saying, come on, give it a rest, Zippy, no wonder it's red.

Now, I don't want to get off on a rant here, but I was viewing a nature documentary on PBS with my son the other night. I wanted to impart into young Simba a sense of awe for the harmony of the cosmos. But as we watched the lion gnawing on a still-breathing gazelle while vultures lingered stoically for their shot at the fly-riddled carrion, it occurred to me that it might be better to install the V chip after all.

Because upon witnessing footage so savage that it would have ended up on Sam Peckinpah's cutting room floor, I recognized that on our worst day humans are eminently more good-natured than animals. Ever see a cat with a mouse? It makes Charlie Manson look like Mike Farrell.

And yet there are people out there, sane, rational beings who insist that humans should render unto animals all the basic rights. Rights, it would appear, ninety-nine percent of humanity doesn't even luxuriate in.

So to be evenhanded, what are some of the specifics of the animal rights argument?

Some claim that animals should not be exploited for entertainment purposes. Activists maintain that show business is demeaning to animals. Hey, it's show business, it's supposed to be demeaning. I don't know if you've noticed, but I'm not exactly doing Ibsen here, all right.

And come to think of it, I'm an animal. Where were the animal rights people when I signed my contract to be in that fucking Rebecca De Mornay film a while back?

You know the animal activists are antifur, and this has caused many fashion designers to now claim that they also are against fur because they care about the plight of animals, especially the ones that have been preapproved for the Platinum Card. Hey, if you designers are so altruistic, why don't you stop having your jeans sewn in Guatemalan sweat shops by fourteen-year-old girls who make twenty dinari for a sixteen-hour day and get to pee less frequently than the guy in the middle seat on a wide-body L-1011 that's heading to sumo camp?

And while we're at it, what makes the fashion industry think that the opinions of these supermodels has more weight or importance simply because they happened to hit the pick six in the genetic lottery?

And by the way, when did supermodels start talking?

And the animal rights lobby also preaches vegetarianism to varying degrees. Look, the philosophy behind shunning meat for moral reasons has more loopholes than Steve Forbes's long form, all right. Animal rights activists believe that as the most evolved carbon-based entity on the planet, we have a responsibility to coexist in harmony with our feathered, finned, and furred pals rather than forcing them to serve our needs.

Yeah, and I'm sure that if I were wandering naked across the Serengeti Plain and happened to come across a pride of lions who were feeling peckish, they'd show me the same fucking courtesy. Come on, in less time than it takes to say "two all-Miller patties" I'd be chili con carnage.

Now, of course there are some commonsense things that we can do right away to improve our relationship with the animal kingdom.

1. Don't feed your dog peanut butter. Unless, of course, the cable goes out for a few seconds.

Dennis Miller

2. After blowing marijuana smoke into your cat's mouth, make sure there is plenty of accessible string nearby.

3. Cockfights are bad. I don't think that there is an American out there who doesn't strongly believe that we need stricter cockfight regulation. I know all of us have taken our kids to the local cockfight and thought, "Man, these basement arenas are just not being kept up." Remember how great cockfights used to be when we were kids? Now they don't even get the names of the cocks right in the program. Cockfighting has just gotten way too commercial.

All right, so much for the dispassionate sarcasm. On the other side of the menu, I mean ledger, I don't think it's right to test cosmetics by trying them on animals first. Bugs Bunny's proclivity for dressing in drag to dupe Elmer Fudd notwithstanding, rabbits as a species aren't especially fond of being forced to wear more makeup than RuPaul at Mardi Gras. However, if we're talking essential medical research that will save human lives, well, I don't give a rat's ass about . . . a rat's ass. You know, if it's between my heart or a gorilla's . . . sorry, Koko. It's been nice signing with you.

The needs of the many outweigh the needs of the few, or the one. That's from *Trek*. Pretty cool, huh?

As long as there are Pomeranians in this country who live better than segments of the two-legged population, the animal rights activists' arguments are about as watertight as the set of *A Night to Remember*.

Call it karma, call it luck of the biological draw, call it whatever you want to call it, Dr. Doolittle, but in the interspecies battle of the bands, humans rock the hardest. Now, get over it.

Of course, that's just my opinion, I could be wrong.

Dennis Miller

Family

___

In Washington recently, a special twelve-person committee was formed to address the problem of teenage pregnancy. You know, there used to be a two-person committee that handled that, it was called parents.

Now, I don't want to get off on a rant here, but family life has never been the *Saturday Evening Post* cover the conservative right would have us believe it once was. I mean, where's the Norman Rockwell painting entitled "Son Announces He's Gay over Easter Ham," or "I Saw Mommy Soul-kissing the Sparkletts Guy," or the classic "Menendez Brothers Give Their Parents a .22-Caliber Explanation As to Why They Didn't Want to Eat Their Vegetables"?

Face it, it ain't the old days. Lucy and Ricky have pushed their beds together and they're doin' it right in front of little Ricky now.

What can I say about today's families? I can say that many inflict the kind of psychic damage on one another that would make John Cassavetes wince.

We've all had that Thanksgiving dinner where your mother regales your date with the story of how difficult you were to toilet-train while you look down at the table and mutter, "You know I'm more fucked than this turkey." Christ, just thinking about it sends me screaming to my therapist for a double session of extended Jungian throwdown.

You know, the American family is more unstable than a hostage situation being negotiated by Crispin Glover. The concept of family is constantly changing. It has been altered more times than Luther Vandross's tuxedo.

My family was *literally* a nuclear family. I don't know about you, but my clan was so dysfunctional, MCI had an administrator on call twenty-four hours a day just to update our Friends and Family package.

Why are families so screwed up? Because for many people, trying to raise children in this economy is like Tom Joad trying to pay the utility bills at San Simeon.

They're struggling because just to stay afloat both parents have to work longer hours. Consequently, children have parents who are more exhausted than Paul Prudhomme bending over to tie his shoelaces.

Y'know, when we look to politicians for answers, what do we get? They parrot the phrase "family values." "Family values" has become a bigger catchall than the front of Rush Limbaugh's shirt after an all-you-can-eat nacho blowout. It's been pounced on to promote school prayer and decry film and TV violence and end the welfare state and attack single mothers. Interestingly enough, the dogs who bark the loudest about family values—Dole, Gingrich, Gramm—all left their first wives. Put that little nugget in your irony hookah and smoke it. These people should pay more attention to their own lives and stop trying to run the lives of others.

Newt Gingrich had an affair while married to his first wife, who had been his high school math teacher, a woman he divorced while she was recuperating from cancer surgery, and then he had to be pursued for adequate child support. Talk about the putz calling the kettle black.

Y'know, we've become a country of "don't do as I do, do as I say." We live in a society where people do more finger-pointing than Bill Clinton at a Dunkin' Donut.

Of course I'm oversimplifying, but that's what I'm paid to do. Look, folks, as troubled as families are, and as troubling as they can be, this essential societal unit must be preserved at all costs. For, you see, the human being is a social creature. Oh, some of us like to think that we're independent loners who enjoy the lives of craggy solitude that we've carved out for ourselves, but then we surround ourselves with a little tribe of like-minded curmudgeons that we can bitch to about what assholes everybody else is.

All I'm saying is never take sides against the family, Fredo. 'Cause it's lonely out there in the rowboat.

Even if your wrists and ankles are raw and chafed from your family ties, just remember, without them, well, who are you?

Your family are the people who cut you the most slack and give you the most chances. I mean, when Richard Dawson says "Name something you find in a refrigerator" and you say "A dictionary" and the rest of America is screaming "You moron" at their TV sets, who's clapping and saying "Good answer! Good answer!"? Your family, that's who.

Families keep everything in perspective. You can grow up, get out in the world, become a big success. You can control fortunes, corner the market, forecast financial trends, steer your company into the twenty-first century and beyond, but you go home to your family and you know who you are? You're just the kid who got tricked by his brothers into drinking a glass of pee.

Of course, that's just my opinion, I could be wrong.

Dennis Miller

Ethnicity

You know, this country is ethnically subdividing
faster than the uranium-235 atoms in Fat Man and
Little Boy. Our pleasantly bubbling societal jambalaya
has boiled over into a provincial brew of suspicion,
intolerance, and plain old not-niceness. Now, I'm not
saying life has to be a fucking Coke commercial, but it
would be great if I could tell a Polish joke once in a
while without a horde of them descending on my house
and unscrewing all my fucking lightbulbs, all right?

Now, I don't want to get off on a rant here, but
when did the contents of our melting pot go from
creamy to super chunk?

You know, if you're going to insist on telling me it's natural for all people of all races and all ethnicities to get along, well, you're living in a fantasy world full of elves and fairies. And, incidentally, elves and fairies didn't get along either.

They hate each other. Elves refer to fairies as "flying Tinker Bell nancy boys," and fairies call elves "rainbow-humping suck pots." You know, really, it should be a constant source of amazement that our country does work on a daily basis and doesn't simply burst into a hundred million separate fistfights. So step out of the Hands Across America line and realize the brutal truth that human beings always have and always will actively look for people to not get along with.

And this is true even within groups—northern Californians don't get along with southern Californians, Irish Catholics don't get along with Irish Protestants, circus clowns fight with birthday party clowns. Begrudging someone else's existence just happens to be the most convenient way to validate your own.

And nowhere are these ego-driven prairie skirmishes more prevalent than in the Tigris and Euphrates of immigration, good old America.

Now, listen, I am all for *legal* immigration. But I am unequivocally against *illegal* immigration. You know why? It's illegal, all right? Where is it written that you can la-di-da across the border at nine A.M. and get your teeth capped for free that afternoon? Fuckin' Canadians.

In addition to immigration, our country also plays host to the United Nations, where the American taxpayer

Dennis Miller

gladly foots the bill for sons of foreign leaders to escape date-rape charges through diplomatic immunity. I must admit, when people from other countries do abuse our largess, I just want to hire a welder to go up the Statue of Liberty and turn that welcoming torch into a giant middle finger.

So I guess I am a little possessive about this great big lug of a country that I call my own. But just a little possessive . . . I'm not gonna play Pin the Blame on the Immigrants for all our country's problems. As a matter of fact, I believe America, much like Keith Richards, thrives on new blood.

Foreigners do not come to this country and take our jobs. Face it, you don't want to be a busboy, or a maid, or the roadside Linus Pauling hawking citrus on the traffic island, or working the overnight shift at the Unocal station breathing gasoline fumes in a booth that's so small it makes the tiger cage in *The Deer Hunter* look like the Taj Mahal. These people are doing jobs that you would never dream of doing.

So get off the immigrants. Truth be told, if you check everybody's family tree, you'd realize that everybody in this nation is an immigrant except for the Indians.

I'm sorry, they're not called Indians anymore, they're called Casino Owner Americans. You know, we are all imported goods, it's just that from day one, people who came here by boat looked down on the people who came here by foot. Why so judgmental, comrades?

Well, America's trivial mentality seems to be made up of equal parts of self-loathing and mistrust of others. Not surprising when you consider that most of us are only a generation or two removed from ancestors who escaped religious and political persecution to find themselves fighting their way up from being the designated bottom-feeders in the New World koi pond of opportunity. But now it's gotten silly. Now we are all isolated in pissed-off little cul-de-sacs of paranoia, guarding our precious wedge of pie from foreign nibbles so jealously that we have lost our ability to enjoy it.

Bottom line. America is a polyglot, bastardized culture. It's been settled by wave after wave of immigrants who assimilated and became part of the establishment so that they could look down their noses at the next wave of immigrants. Therein lies the paradox of this great land of ours: Freedom of belief also means freedom to make fun of the 7-Eleven guy's sandals, all right?

But poking fun is one thing and exclusionary discrimination another, and if we're not gonna walk the walk, it's time to take down Lady Liberty, which, by the way, was a gift from the stinky French, and replace her with the doorman from the Roxbury. Remember, xenophobia doesn't benefit anybody unless you're playing high-stakes Scrabble.

On the other side of the coin, be it rupee, the drachma, the peso, baksheesh, or wampum, the favor of inclusion deserves the courtesy of assimilation.

Make the effort. It's poor party manners to come to live in this country and then have a hissy fit because the parking signs aren't posted in Hmong, okay? And, uh, don't get uptight because your college is teaching courses on Emerson and Thoreau instead of seventeenth-century

Dennis Miller

Javanese goatherd poets, all right? Don't take your kid out of school because her third-grade class made colored Easter eggs but didn't conduct any druid rituals. You're in America now, so open the closet door and start hanging up your pants and shirts.

Yeah, this country's founding fathers are a bunch of dead rich white men, but they did set things up so you could come and sit at the table, so don't piss in the finger bowls, all right? Thank you. In return for unfettered economic opportunity and no government death squads, try to get along with your new stepmotherland, and don't be resentful if there's a set of house rules already in place.

Go with the flow. Pay your taxes. Speak the language. Garlic is not a cologne. And for Christ's sake, left lane fast, right lane slow.

Of course, that's just my opinion, I could be wrong.

Are Movies
Getting Worse?

Well, I see my film *Murder at 1600* is now playing
at the budget theater across the street on a double bill
with *Benji Gets Stuck on a Leg.* And my other opus,
Bordello of Blood, you may remember, was in theaters
for one weekend and then hopped on a turbo-rocket
sled to the ninety-nine-cent bin. So, uh, who better
than me to dim the lights, part the velvet curtains, and
project some flickering images about the current state
of the movies. And, hopefully, the audience will
be listening.

Now, I don't want to get off on a rant here, but
between test audiences, exit polls, and focus groups,
the creative filmmaking process is now about as
spontaneous and inspired as a Jesse Helms
bowel movement.

Be honest, how many times have you gone to a multi-screen theater complex and just stood there, looking up at the marquees, trying to decide which movie sucked the least?

And today's moviegoing experience is no joy itself. To all the moviegoers out there who think the term "talkie" refers to them, shut your blathering pie hole. Okay? Just because coincidentally the first time you ever told the actor up on the screen "Don't go in there," the actor didn't go in there . . . that doesn't mean the actor actually heard you, okay. It would have happened anyway. I can guarantee you nowhere in the film's script does it say "Jerkoff in the audience who everybody hates decides what happens next." All right? So just sit back, stuff your fat fuck face with popcorn, and watch the film.

And what's with the dancing candy film they run before the movie starts, huh? If the candy can dance, and, for that matter, play musical instruments, why should I get up, go to the snack bar, and buy the candy? Why can't it just walk down the fucking aisle and meet me at my seat, okay? Let's go, goobers, put down the trombone, come here, and let me eat you. And this is the nineties. Can't we get a condom on that hot dog that jumps into the bun, for Christ's sake, okay?

And why is it that the Coke costs more than the tickets? You see, that's how they get you. They serve you a cup of Coke so large, Ted Kennedy could drop a fucking Oldsmobile into it, which means halfway through the movie you're so bloated you have to step outside for twenty minutes of dialysis, which means you have to come back the next day and see the movie again to find out the part you missed.

And unless the rating of the movie I'm watching contains more Xs than Dick Weber's bowling score sheet, the floor should not be sticky. Okay? I've been to some theaters where before you sit down you have to decide where you want your feet to be throughout the movie, because once you set them on that floor, that's where they're at, okay. And at the end of the movie it's just easier to step out of your shoes and leave them behind.

And have you noticed that as the popcorn bags get bigger, the screens get smaller? You know what I think? I think they ought to make the entire plane out of the stuff they make the black box out of.

I leave a movie now, I'm in the lobby buying T-shirts, coffee mugs, videos, beach towels, and Willem Dafoe bendable, live-action figures. You know, the only part of the movie I'm not buying is the plot.

And that leads us to the films themselves. These days, by the time a story is actually made into a movie, it has been passed around like a goatskin flask at a Blue Oyster Cult concert. The script has been exposed to more secondhand guessing than schizophrenics week on *Jeopardy!*

And you know something? Hollywood's solution is to always throw more money at the problem. Now, last year, a lot of low-budget films were up for the Academy Awards, so you know what that means. That means this year Hollywood will be making a lot of low-budget films . . . for a hundred million dollars.

But here are some much simpler ways Hollywood can make better films.

Dennis Miller

First up, instead of twenty independent films coming out each year that make us feel guilty because we can't see them all, save us the hassle, make one huge movie. Like last year, wouldn't it have been so much better if there was one big film about a retarded chain-smoking burn victim who crashed his plane in the desert then has a nervous breakdown after trying to learn how to play the piano and eat french fried potaters at the same time so he moves to Fargo, North Dakota, and befriends a young boy by stuffing his abusive stepfather into a wood chipper and then at the end of the film he is shown the money?

Secondly, the end of every Merchant-Ivory film should be accompanied by the following announcement: All right, ladies, you now owe your man some head.

And finally, the most moronic thing about modern movies has to be the catch phrase, the little signature line a performer feels he needs to use as a Pavlovian pork chop to wave in front of his devoted audience. It's just disrespectful to use some tired old hackneyed phrase as a lame crutch.

Of course, that's just my opinion, I could be wrong.

The Armed Forces

Does anybody remember how innocent being in the service was in Gomer's days, huh?

Now, I don't want to get off on a rant here, but it appears our military has become an overpriced 4-H Club rife with hazing, homophobia, harassment, and hypocrisy and a hopeless money pit dug ever deeper with million-dollar shovels and billion-dollar buckets.

I know we need the military. I know that without them, America has enemies who'd be down on us like Luciano Pavarotti on a ballpark frank. And when I talk about the military, I am not speaking about the regular Joes, the men and women who have given their lives for this country or the millions who have served honorably. I have to speak to the people who run the military—the generals, the Congress, and the squares in the Pentagon.

I know what you're saying. You're saying, "Dennis, you were never in the military, how can you criticize it?" Well, first, neither was the commander in chief, but that doesn't stop him from running it. Second, I, like the rest of you, am paying for it. And third, because my grandfather was the guy Patton slapped in that tent. You know, my grandfather on the other side had a military connection too. He was LeBeau's lighting stand-in on *Hogan's Heroes*.

Now, the first thing they do when you join the armed forces is strip you of any personal identity and make you indistinguishable from everybody around you. It's sort of like getting a sitcom on network television.

For many people the military provides an option for a career when you can't figure out the fryolater at Denny's. You aren't doing that well in school, you're in trouble with the law, and you need some discipline.

So the recruiter drops by the high school you're at and shows you the brochures about shooting big guns and going to exotic lands. The next thing you know, they're shaving your head at an indoctrination center in Twiddle-Your-Ball-Sack, South Carolina, getting you up at four A.M. to take ten-mile hikes in the rain with a pack on your back containing a hyperactive midget while the drill instructor screams at you that he's about to rip your eye out and fuck the socket. By the way, the Socket Fuckers happens to be the name of our show's softball team. Trust me, you don't even want to see the mascot.

Now, the military's called the "armed" forces, but you know, with all the scandals of late, perhaps there's a more appropriate appendage to use as a description.

If the recent deluge of sexual-misconduct incidents is any indication, behind the spit-shine pomp of the military facade, the armed forces is just one big Benny Hill sketch with everybody chasing each other around in double time with their pants around their ankles. Christ, the stories oozing out of the Pentagon these days couldn't be more libidinous if the Joint Chiefs of Staff were Larry Flynt, Bob Guccione, Billy Idol, and Caligula.

A question that's been bandied about a lot the last few years is "Should there be gays in the military?" Now, first, there are already a lot of gays in the military. I mean, you don't get that many men all living together to be that neat and tidy just by discipline alone. Okay? And secondly, forget the gays, lately the heterosexuals have been the ones, uh, shall we say, firing their weapons at unauthorized targets.

Besides, there's a long, proud tradition of gays serving in our military. I saw those looks Captain Binghamton was always giving McHale all along. That look that said "You know, I'm mad at you, Clint, but I can't stay mad at you." If you think *McHale's Navy* was a sitcom about a group of misfits defying authority, you're wrong. It was a love story, Fuji.

Military service offers great opportunities for women. Where else can you be raped by your commanding officer and then be court-martialed because while it was happening you didn't call him sir? You know, from Tailhook to the Aberdeen Proving Grounds, women have fared about as well in the military as a balsa-wood chair in Luciano Pavarotti's dressing room. And it's not surprising when you take into account the fact that for thousands of years, and up until very recently, females were categorized in the

Dennis Miller

military mind under the heading Spoils of War, mere objects to be carried off and defiled as proof of your forces' superiority. Undoing centuries' worth of conditioning, as recent events have borne out, is going to be as easy as getting Janet Reno into a size four catsuit.

And this recent episode with Lieutenant Kelly Flinn being discharged proves that men aren't responsible for all the sexual shenanigans in the service. Kelly Flinn was stupid. If she wanted to get away with adultery, she should have fucked a general. Okay?

So why has the military gone completely to hell lately? Well, one big problem is that I think the names army, navy, air force, and marines are just too tame, too old-school. To perk things up a bit, may I suggest the following more impressive and scarier name changes: army—Murder, Incorporated; navy—Aqua Kill 3000; air force—The Dead Foreigner Squad; and the marines—The Fighting O.J.'s.

Of course, that's just my opinion, I could be wrong.

Smoking

You know, they say every cigarette you smoke makes your life seven minutes shorter, and I know that's true because I had an uncle, and the first cigarette he ever smoked was on an airplane. Smoked the cigarette, and he immediately dropped dead of a heart attack. Seven minutes later, the plane crashed into a mountain.

Now, I don't want to get off on a rant here, but America's attitude about smoking has become more hostile than a militia member at a tax audit. These days even the Philip Morris employee cafeteria has a no smoking section. If you walked into a restaurant and loudly demanded that they serve you a charbroiled live puppy, you'd probably cause less of an outcry than you would by simply sitting down and lighting up a smoke.

When I say "smoke," I'm talking mostly about cigarettes, although I guess with the increasing popularity of
cigars, we have to include them in this discussion. For
years, cigars concerned only half the population, but their
usage is growing more prevalent with the fairer sex. For
women, smoking cigars is like going to Chippendale's:
You're basically saying, "Look, guys, we can be just as big
a bunch of assholes as you can."

Now, it's been proven that tobacco company execu-
tives' sworn congressional testimony concerning the addictive properties of nicotine had all the sincerity of a
defense attorney's tie rack. But who can possibly be
shocked by this?

Tobacco companies will stop at nothing to win the
smoking wars. Now their scientists are saying some of the
smoking research data is no longer valid because the contemporary mores dictate that rats have to step outside
their mazes to have the smoke.

Hey, don't blame the cigarette makers. Tobacco companies are being sued way too much. I admit they're evil
poison-mongers who give other evil poison-mongers a bad
name. Yes, they lie about the addictive nature of their
products and get rich doing it. But come on, tell the truth,
we knew they were lying all along. If you're saying you
didn't know cigarettes were bad for you, you're lying
through that hole in your trachea. Of course it causes
lung cancer. Of course it causes emphysema. *It's fucking
smoke.* Would you build a campfire and every hour stand
real close and take deep breaths? How could you not
know smoking is bad for you? Is having teeth the color of
caramel corn *normal*? Is coughing up your lungs one
smoldering loogie at a time normal? God gave you two

lungs, so don't be an asshole. Think. Use one lung for smoking and the other one for breathing.

Here are some signs that it might be time to quit smoking:

1. Before lighting up, you wrap a nicotine patch around your cigarette.

2. Your newborn twin sons are named Benson and Hedges.

3. You name each cigarette and have a personal conversation with it while you smoke.

4. You're at Arlington Cemetery, paying your respects to JFK, and you lean over and light one up off the eternal flame.

And 5. You shit pure tar.

Listen, the bottom line on cigarette smoking is it's really just the way you interpret things. I mean, they say smoking gives you cancer. Sure, you can be negative and look at that as a bad thing, or you can see that smoking *gives* you cancer. It *gives* it to you. It's a present. Here, here's cancer. . . . Why, thank you very much, Mr. Cigarette.

You know, when I find myself in a room where everyone's smoking, and it gets too intense, you know what I do? I don't start waving my hand around and fake coughing; I don't start rattling off heart disease and lung cancer stats like some autistic surgeon general; I don't lecture anybody about their lifestyle choices. . . . I leave the room, okay? My acceptance of smokers is one of the compromises, one of the little negotiations that one must make if one is to live in modern urban society.

I don't know why people complain about secondhand smoke. At nearly two dollars a pack, don't you realize how much money they're saving you?

Plus, if you smoke, you get to read matchbook covers and learn about the exciting career opportunities awaiting you in cartooning.

And hey to all you militant antismokers whom I see screaming at strangers for lighting up: If you were that concerned about your lungs, what in the fuck are you doing living in L.A.?

Of course, that's just my opinion, I could be wrong.

Acting

There are plans in the Los Angeles area to open three new oxygen bars where people can unwind and breathe pure oxygen. Yeah, that's just what people in L.A. need, more air in their heads.

Christ, everybody in L.A. is either an actor or allowing one to sleep on their couch. Now, I don't want to get off on a rant here, but as I tee off on acting, it's not an across-the-boards condemnation. Meryl Streep is a genius. Paul Scofield is an artist. I'm not talking about them and people like them. I'm talking about bad actors who take themselves way too seriously. You know, the ones who refer to their bodies as their instrument. Instrument, my ass . . . Believe me, you'll know bad acting when you see it. Acting is bad if while you're watching it you're thinking, "Did I leave the iron on?"

With all the tedious, humiliating, stupid ways there are to make a living in this world, why do so many people choose acting? Maybe they didn't get enough attention as a child, maybe they watched too much television, or maybe they saw a movie I was in and said, "Come on, Miller does it, how hard can it be?" Acting is a constant exercise in humiliation. A "how low can you go" limbo game where it helps to have a double-jointed ego because it's going to be bent, stretched, and forced into positions a lanky yogi on roofies couldn't manage. You come to Hollywood to ply your craft and you get a job waiting tables at Der Wienerschnitzel in Culver City so you can network with Sony interns as they ask you to refill the relish tub.

You join an improv troupe called Can o' Nuts and perform in the basement of the Unitarian Church in Van Nuys with the half son of the guy who was the voice on the intercom in *Rhoda.* Eventually, you audition for Tom Arnold's new sitcom, and the director is Anson Williams, who played Potsie on *Happy Days,* and he believes you need to tighten up your skills a little. So you take an acting class from the guy who ran the bookstore in *Banacek.* You like the class so much, you exhaust your nest egg taking it and eventually you end up back home, where you teach a movement theory class at the local community college. And in Hollywood, that would be considered "making it." Okay?

Now, if you're a woman in Hollywood, it's off to the plastic surgeon for, of course, a breast reduction. Because, as everyone knows, there are no acting jobs for women with large breasts.

Male Hollywood producers are among the most cultured, refined, and spiritual men in the world. They don't want to see how you look in a bikini or a white tube top or even topless doing jumping jacks. They just want to see if you can act. And acting, if nothing else, is living in the "now." For most aspiring actors, it goes something like this: "Now I'm broke. Now I'm still broke. Now I'm going to sell my blood so I can buy some ramen noodles." A lot of people will say after seeing my movies that I don't act, I just play myself. Nothing could be further from the truth. It's just that the characters I create are so transparent, you can see me inside of them. Actually, acting is all about pretending, and in my case I pretend that I know how to act.

After I get the part, how do I approach the script? The first thing I do is ask myself what does this character want? Of course, that's an impossible question to answer, so I have to ask myself what do I want? And that answer is very simple. I want to get home before six. So then I essentially ask myself, what does this guy have to do and say in order for me to be already in my undies by the time *SportsCenter* starts.

Actors are always talking about their motivation, that is, what makes their character do the things he does. Well, for all of my plum roles I used a special acting technique for my motivation that I call the check method. See, in every one of my movies, my "character" knew that when the filming was done, I would get a big check, which I would cash in for a stack of green rectangles that I could exchange for food to put in my children's headholes.

And speaking of children, I'd like to say to any parent out there who's thinking of putting their child in the movies: Fuck you, okay? Don't destroy their lives hauling them from one wretched audition to another just because you don't feel like supporting the family yourself. Anyone who's thinking of putting their kids in the movies, I have two words for you: Mickey Rooney.

Listen, acting is unique to the human species. Role-playing is often essential to the successful negotiation of a day-to-day life. Acting is dishonesty squared. It is the instinct of deception schooled, practiced, and honed to the point of a journey-level trade, where it is further worked and prodded until it is hopefully raised to an art form. At that moment the irony kicks in, the dog catches its tail, and pure acting becomes one of the most elemental embodiments of human truth. The actor becomes a selfless, agendaless vessel for the thoughts and emotions of a character born of a collision of ink and paper, incorruptible because its . . . its . . . because of its . . . aw, shit! Line!

Of course, that's just my opinion, I could be wrong.

Sobriety

The sobriety craze has got a tighter grip on our collective consciousness than Bill Clinton's hand on a civil servant's ass.

Now, I don't want to get off on a rant here, but since when is day-to-day life so goddamn wonderful that we're not entitled to help ourselves to the occasional edge-blurring liquid anaesthetic?

In the late twentieth century, staying sober has become just as much an addiction as getting wasted. Between therapists, 12-step programs, and Prozac, we buzz-loving Americans approach staying on the wagon with the same over-the-top zeal we use to fall off it. It's gotten to the point that people can't even use moderation in moderation.

Now, I'm not trying to trivialize the nightmare that is addiction. It's a difficult thing when you start to notice that someone close to you has a drinking problem. You see the little signs, like when they ask the waitress what wine goes with a grand slam breakfast. Or when they go to a liquor store and bring their own handtruck. Or when they walk up and down the bar pointing at people's drinks, asking, "Are you gonna finish that?"

I realize that some people get dealt a lousy genetic hand. I'm sure there are some physical predispositions to alcohol abuse—maybe lacking certain chemicals in your brain, maybe a problem with your metabolism, maybe just being a Kennedy.

So I'll agree that there can be a hereditary template for alcoholism. I'll even go so far as to call it a disease, like I'm supposed to. But you know, folks, in all honesty, if you have to have a disease, this is definitely the one you want to have. I mean, what other disease do you get pretzels and chicken wings with?

Besides, the cause of this disease is not only known, it is the root word of the disease itself, alcohol. If you avoid it, it will avoid you. Hey, face it, wouldn't it be much harder to stir up compassion for lymphoma victims if they got it from years of repeatedly chugging ice cold cans of something called cancer juice?

Many people go for decades without addressing their steadily worsening problem. Occasional cracks in their armor may leave them shaken but not stirred to action. Others, however, get tired of French-kissing the gutter drain and join Alcoholics Anonymous.

I think that Alcoholics Anonymous is truly a wonderful, lifesaving organization. And privacy is of the utmost importance in AA and members are very, very serious about protecting their anonymity. If you don't believe me, just tap on the window of someone with a "One Day at a Time" or a "Do It Sober" bumper sticker and ask them.

But maybe that's an L.A. thing, because it's becoming a tad trendy out here to proselytize about your personal rebirth. I just think regular folk are beginning to tire of stories of celebrities checking into the Betty Ford Clinic for fourteen minutes to undo the damage incurred from years and years of having your ass unduly kissed by everybody around you just because you played Señor Couscous, the wacky neighbor with a dark past and a third nipple, on some shit sitcom for a season and a half.

In a nutshell, when you join AA, you acknowledge that your life has become unmanageable and you are powerless over your addiction. Then you start going to meetings around the clock, drinking so much coffee, Juan Valdez names his fucking donkey after you, and smoking cigarettes like Dennis Leary in the waiting room of the maternity ward. You also participate in a 12-step recovery program, one of the steps being to make amends to the people in your life for the hurt you caused them while you were drinking. Yeah, like I need to be reminded.

Look, if you're someone I know and you're getting sober and you think you wronged me once and you feel compelled to track me down so you can make amends . . . don't, okay? You're not doing it for me, you're doing it for you. And if you absolutely must make amends to me, at least wait until *I'm* drunk so I won't have to remember any of it the next day.

Dennis Miller

Anyone in AA will tell you that first and foremost, you have to admit to having a problem. Here are some blurred signposts that might signal you're weaving down the road to alcoholism.

1. If you walked out of the movie *Leaving Las Vegas* early because it made you thirsty.

2. If Boris Yeltsin asks for your autograph.

3. If your designated driver is Kelsey Grammer.

4. If you have to paint the words "don't panic, you're at home" on the ceiling above your bed.

And finally, you really know you have a drinking problem if, when you go to buy bathroom floor tile, you press it to your face to see how comfortable it would be to sleep on.

Of course, that's just my opinion, I could be wrong.

Violence
in Media

Now, I don't want to get off on a rant here, but there's a lot of violence in the media today. And I think we all know the core issue that we must confront as a nation. Without a doubt, Jimmy Carter must be brought in to mediate between the Road Runner and Wile E. Coyote, because this Sicilian thing has got to stop.

In an increasingly permissive and shockproof society, where taboos are being shattered like a bank of TV sets at Graceland during a Robert Goulet special, we have all become more desensitized than Rush Limbaugh's ass after an eighteen-hour bus ride.

This is an issue that concerns me deeply, because I, personally, am a victim of media violence. Every movie I'm in, I get killed halfway through. I'm like the guy on *Star Trek* in the red shirt.

Now, to listen to the frantic bleatings of social reformers and family-values-mongers, you'd think that media violence is some new, demonic invention and before that pesky Quentin Tarantino came along we were skipping through an idyllic G-rated wonderland. Well, guess what? From cave drawings depicting the hunt to tribal war songs to a gory little tome called the Bible, the portrayal of violence has, in one way or another, been a part of human discourse ever since we stopped dragging our knuckles on the ground and started using them to give each other noogies.

But we're hypocritical about violence in the media. We're looking for someone to blame if our kid goes bad, and the media is a defenseless target for the clusterfuck of self-righteous rhetoric that passes for intelligent debate these days. We all seem to want our children to watch nothing but nice, positive stories so that they'll be so suffused with love, they'll go traipsing through the world, handing out big flowers to strangers like the summer of love hippie kids who always placed a daffodil in Jack Webb's gun barrel on *Dragnet*. The truth is, TV isn't the biggest influence on your kids. You are. There's probably more real emotional violence and bad vibes at the average American family dinner table than in an entire season of *Highlander*, not to mention better acting.

Mom and Dad, look, your television is not a babysitter. It can't rack up long distance calls talking to its boyfriend who's away at college, it can't eat the frozen

Wolfgang Puck pizza you were saving for the De La Hoya pay per view, and it can't have a six-year fling with a Kennedy. It's just a machine.

I don't even know if I really buy that there's a connection between violent TV and violent behavior. I mean, I grew up watching a steady diet of *Mannix,* Krazy Kat cartoons, and *Combat,* and I'm so nonconfrontational, I make Deepak Chopra look like Oddjob.

Besides, it seems to me, as far as adults go, we gobble up TV violence like it's an ear and we're a mentally unbalanced boxer.

Just look at the titles of the sickening shows that prey on our morbid curiosity: *When Animals Kill, Brushes with Death,* and one of the worst of all, *Circus of the Stars.* And, come on, when you watch *Circus of the Stars,* aren't you rooting for Richard Mulligan to fall off the high wire, ricochet off Tootie from *The Facts of Life,* and then crush Screech?

What about the local news? In reporting violent crime, the local news comports itself with all the dignity and responsibility of Moe, Larry, and Shemp locked in a haunted house.

And network news shows aren't much better. The big three all feel the ratings pressure, and know that if they shovel some bloody chum onto the airwaves, Americans will swim over to their little pond and gorge themselves on the carcass. I mean, do we really need *Dateline NBC* on four hours every night, combing through every detail of some horrible act of violence like Columbo with obsessive-compulsive disorder? And while we're on the subject:

The only thing stiffer than Stone Phillips is Richard Sim-
mons watching him.

Hey, this is all very simple. Forget V-chips, forget government intervention, forget blaming it on the networks
and get back to basics. If you don't like what's on, you
have the power. To all my fellow men out there lying in
bed watching TV, take a look down. . . . You see that
thing you're holding in your hand? Well, let go of it, pick
up the remote control, and watch what you want.

Of course, that's just my opinion, I could be wrong.

Hype

Boy, the whole Barney phenomenon has tapered off a little, hasn't it? Do you remember the hype on that creature when he first emerged from the tar pit?

Now, I don't want to get off on a rant here, but if the media doesn't stop trying to bludgeon me into believing that their designated Flavor of the Nanosecond is about to be the Next Big Thing, I'm going to have to put on my lambada shoes and kick some Yahoo Serious ass.

From politics to sports to show business, the world has airbrushed away all expectations of quality and instead relies on ballyhoo instead of substance. If P. T. Barnum were alive today, he would be spearheading a campaign for truth in advertising.

Now, what exactly is hype? Well, hype is the glittering rhinestone on the jumpsuit of mediocrity that catches our eye and makes us think, "Hey, maybe the Spice Girls don't suck." It's the triumph of style over substance, predicated on the sad truth that most of us, if the gift-wrapping on the outside of the box is fancy enough, won't notice that inside there's nothing but a big pile of shit.

Why are we so susceptible to hype? Well, it's simple really. We're stupid and lazy. We want to be led. We want to be told what is desirable. We want to be flattered. It is amazing how little care a weed needs to take root in the fertile rot of the compost heaps that are our brains. Are you with me on this, folks?

Hype is everywhere in our society, on every level. It starts at the top with our promoter in chief, the man from Hype—Bill Clinton. Clinton has done more for spin than Brian Boitano with an inner ear infection in a fucking centrifuge. You know, if Clinton blows any more smoke up my ass, my sphincter is going to sue Philip Morris.

And it's not only politics. Just look at the way they hype bad movies in their ads by editing the reviews. It's ridiculous. Like the reviewer would say "Whoever made this movie should be put in a gas chamber" and in the ad the quote is simply ". . . a gas!"

Another example of how hype has worked on me— Matthew McConaughey. I love him. I absolutely love the guy, and I have no idea who he is. I haven't seen one movie he's been in, yet I think he might be the finest actor of our generation. You know what else I know? I know that he likes four-wheel-drive vehicles, he has a golden retriever, and he likes to get out of L.A. to clear his head. I have no fucking idea how I know all this about a guy who I don't know, but I just think he's fantastic. I really do.

And you know I don't want to hear another word about the Internet or the Web or chat rooms or flame wars or information superhighways or any other trumped-up jag-off computer term.

I mean, "surfin" the Net? How is sitting at your computer for hours on end banging keys like Lancelot Link's piano player remotely connected to surfing?

Now, last year there was a celestial load of hype surrounding Mars. While I'm all for a certain amount of scientific exploration, this is way out of hand. Mars is. Is it really important to anybody except a bunch of Buzz Lightweight guys from the A.V. Squad? I mean, we didn't learn anything that's going to improve our lives in any way. We've spent billions of dollars so a robot could hump rocks that a bunch of geeks argued whether to call Snagglepuss or Secret Squirrel. I mean, what is the big deal? You know why it's the red planet? It was embarrassed by all the undeserved attention.

Then there is Dennis Rodman. The Sistine Ceiling of hype. Dennis Rodman wouldn't be the star he is today if it weren't for hype. He's always been a solid player, but come on, being the leading rebounder in the league is like playing first chair tuba in the Des Moines Pops.

You'll always work, but you're not gonna get laid. Okay? Unless, of course, you dye your hair to resemble the muted rainbow hue of bad meat, sport so many tattoos that Maori warriors cringe at you, and get so many body piercings that you whistle eight different tunes when you ride a bike.

Mike Tyson's suspended in the U.S., so how soon do you think before Don King starts advertising his come-back fight in another country? What do you think this angle's going to be? "The Bite on the Isle of Wight"? "Can You Hear in Zaire"? "Lobes in Manitobe"? Huh? It's coming.

To try and keep from falling victim to advertising hype, ask yourself this simple question: Should I really care what kind of beer frogs recommend?

Listen, just accept the fact that hype is here to stay because we live in an increasingly narcissistic universe that everyone believes they're the center of.

It's that sort of self-involvement that even has people like Liz Taylor and Michael Jordan coming out with their own fragrances. Hey, big deal, we all have our own fragrance, they're called farts. We all just don't put them in a bottle. Okay?

Of course, that's just my opinion, I could be wrong.

The American
Education System

Now, I don't want to get off on a rant here, but
today's American educational system, quite frankly,
ain't doing so goodly or goodish. This country's
public schools couldn't be more poorly funded and
badly directed if the secretary of education were
Ed Wood.

If you're lucky enough that you can afford a private
school, then much of what follows probably won't make
sense to you, because unfortunately the majority of the
problems are in the public schools, the ones called
P.S., which is appropriate because they're treated as
an afterthought.

Our public school system has become a giant mono-lithic substitute teacher, an overworked and underpaid civil servant with an impossible load on its back and a huge "kick me" sign on its ass. And if our public school system isn't a giant monolithic substitute teacher, then my name isn't Peter Goesinya or Dick Hertz or Phil Mc-Crackup or Joe Pendulous Balls.

Well, anyway, this decline in our school system is hav-ing a discernible effect. I can tell that my audiences aren't quite as educated as they used to be. You know I like to salt my remarks with references to the best of Victorian literature, but I'm just not getting the response I once did with such pithy observations like "Christ, looking to Clin-ton for moral leadership is like Samuel Johnson getting style tips from Lord Bulwer-Lytton." You know, if our high schools don't start doing their jobs, I'm going to have to resort to something desperate, like trying to get laughs just by saying the word "motherfucker."

It seems to me that if we don't step up to the black-board and solve the problems facing this country's educa-tional system, we might as well use the chalk to draw an outline around the future of America's kids.

You know, maybe I'm not the best guy to be address-ing the subject of education. Frankly, when I was in school, I generated more C's than a Spanish couple reaching simultaneous orgasm. But the subject of our public schools hits very close to my heart. For years I have been earnestly contributing vast amounts to the Califor-nia school system. That's right. I'm a lottery player.

In days gone by, schools used to be orderly one-room red houses where kids would eagerly learn how to use impressive phrases like "in days gone by." But today schools are replete with acts of violence that make what Tyson did to Holyfield look like Richie Cunningham giving one of the Hooper triplets a hickey. Yes, the gun, the ultimate hall pass. Anybody remember when the only time lead flew in school was when somebody threw a pencil?

Violence and intimidation are such accepted parts of school for many kids these days that when the teacher tells students to raise their hands, just out of force of habit, they raise both of them.

But I guess we should just be thankful that teachers dare to tell children anything nowadays. You see, being a teacher these days is not limited to the boring educational stuff anymore. Noooo. You get to do so much more than just teach. You're a one-man SWAT team, confiscating an AK-47 here, defusing a lunch box pipe bomb there.

And then you're so burnt out by the time you reach the après-school parent/teacher meetings, you explode and tell some parents that they can take the college money they've been saving and buy themselves a cigarette boat because the only college their little Slappy is going to has the word "beauty" or "clown" in front of it.

And as far as a retreat from the maelstrom of malevolent and misdirected mayhem, what do the teachers have? Well, they have the teachers' lounge. Oooh, what a lush oasis that is. A twenty-by-twenty Serbian bunker strewn with furniture the cast of *Trainspotting* would pass on that's filled with so much smoke, you'd swear Marge Schott just elected a new pope.

Dennis Miller

But can you blame teachers? We're sending them into battle unarmed. In many instances it appears that schools have softened the curriculum so that no one feels like they're left behind. And that depletion of expectation in the end works against the children. Too often now, teachers have to grade on curves that would make Anna Nicole Smith look like Olive Oyl.

But the curriculum is fixable. Obviously the biggest part of America's educational problem is that after school kids go home to parents who are more involved in their tan than they are in their child's education. Hey, folks, it's not a fluff-and-fold situation where you drop off the kid and zap, you pick him up twelve years later and he can carry on a conversation with Stephen Hawking.

If you're not happy with the way your kids are learning, it might be time to do a quick check on the home environment to make sure you're providing them with optimal conditions. For instance, does your teenage daughter put her kids to bed at a reasonable hour so she can study?

Of course, that's just my opinion, I could be wrong.

Bad Drivers

A new law in Arkansas makes it illegal to drive under the speed limit in the left-hand lane. Yeah, like there's a fucking fast lane in Arkansas.

Actually, I think Arkansas should be applauded for such a commonsense driving statute. Because our roads, quite frankly, have turned into an imbecilic cyclotron of disparate particle brains supercolliding into one another at the speed of litigation. Now, I don't want to get off on a rant here, but every time I go for a drive nowadays, I get the feeling that every other motorist on the road has made me their unwitting partner in some bizarre murder-suicide pact.

And I speak from experience. I drive ninety miles each way to and from work, and the sad thing is, I live only four miles away.

But I'll tell you, the next time I do my taxes, I'm allowing for depreciation due to wear and tear on my middle finger.

Now, I know that at least part of the reason there are so many bad drivers in L.A. is because mass transit just isn't an option here. I don't know about you guys, but if you've ever had to wait at a bus stop out there, you're painfully aware of the need to get your own set of wheels to avoid sitting next to the guy who wants to show you the human thumb he has in a Baggie.

There are also too many tourists driving around southern California. And you know a tourist with the full collision waiver on a rented Chevy Lumina is like a kamikaze pilot who just got a Dear John letter.

Hey, I wouldn't trust half the people in L.A. behind a potter's wheel much less a steering column. All right? Just once I'd like to be able to run down to the quiki mart without having to swerve into a ditch trying to avoid Stanley Tucci's ex-publicist steering a Porsche with his knees while he's facedown in a laptop surfing the Net for instructions how to operate his newly installed passenger side hibachi.

Driving in L.A. you get cut off more frequently than Teddy Kennedy bar-hopping on St. Patrick's Day, and the flow of traffic on the 405 makes Strom Thurmond's urethra look like Splash Mountain.

Here's a message to every Los Angeles driver who's ever been in front of me at a light trying to make a left turn—*GO!* Just go! You can make it! You've got a mile and a half till that car gets here! A five-hundred-pound guy on roller skates using only the power of a slight breeze to propel him could make it, so just fucking GO!

Anyway, no wonder people can't drive, look who taught them—the high school driver's ed instructor, who was generally whoever drew the short straw between the football coach, the typing teacher, and Gladys, the chain-smoking cafeteria lady with the lazy eye.

What probably doesn't help matters is that drivers' licenses are almost as easy to get as People's Choice Award nominations. You know, if you've ever been in line at the DMV and eavesdropped on some of the Franz-Kafka-by-the-way-of-Charlene-Tilton conversations taking place, you begin to wonder how people manage to transport themselves without producing more casualties than there are in the director's cut of *Reservoir Dogs*.

But not all drivers are dangerous. No, that would be too easy. In addition to the dangerous ones, we have the sub-species Mobilus Moronus, the annoying driver. Hey, I don't care what you do in front of me. Just do it fast, okay, Chim-Chim?

And what about the people who transverse the entire Gadsden Purchase with their turn signal on? What do you think that clicking sound is, assface? What do you think that is? The gnashing of vertebrae in that tattered pipe cleaner you call a brain stem? Obviously, the same primal instinct is at work here that compelled our ancestors to keep the fire burning at all times lest it go out, because no one but the shaman had the magic to bring the fire back to life, and if they switch off their turn signal, what if they want to make it go on again? They'll have to go all the way back to the dealership and beseech the merchant of the iron horses to impart the secret of the turn-signal switch to them.

And if you're one of those people who can't be bothered with turn signals, listen: I've got enough to worry about in my life without having to do a fucking Vulcan mind-meld on some jagoff like you in a Geo Storm ahead of me.

You know what? You know what we should do? We should use that "Baby on Board" thing as a point of departure and have asshole stickers. A small stick-on appliqué of a human rectum seated behind the wheel of a cute little bummobile. All right? We see somebody make an asshole move, we get to mark their car with an asshole sticker that's harder to get off than Miss Hathaway during banking hours. You get three asshole stickers in any given calendar year and you can't drive anymore. And don't whine to me. . . . Do not whine to me about "how am I going to get around if I can't drive a car?" Hey, do what everybody else does who's not allowed to drive anymore. Become a pilot for Valu-Jet.

Of course, that's just my opinion, I could be wrong.

Computers

This computer thing is out of hand. Christ, now I got abacus salesmen using computers. It's beyond comprehension. Now, I don't want to get off on a rant here, but, as anyone who has ever tried to purchase a PC knows, computer technology moves faster than Luciano Pavarotti going after a cinnabun. No matter what computer you buy, no matter how much you spend, by the time you get it to your car, it's an eight-track tape player.

True, computers have made it possible for us to do our jobs much more quickly and efficiently. And what do we do with our newly acquired scads of leisure time? We play Nintendo till our thumbs bleed, we sit on-line for hours in chat rooms, participating in imbecilic exchanges with people we wouldn't be caught dead talking to in person, and we spend the entire morning on hold with an automated teller because the ATM machine somehow believes that we're now more overdrawn than M. C. Escher's doodle pad.

Just when did all this computer stuff happen anyway? You know, one day I was playing Pong, the next thing I know Wes, the gas meter guy with the eye patch, has an uplink to a satellite on his tool belt.

They say the cars of the future will be equipped with dashboard computers complete with maps and a global positioning device. Hey, listen, I'm going to the store for milk, I'm not fucking Magellan tacking around the Cape of Good Hope, all right? Tell me, O global positioning device, where can Ponce De Dennis locate the 7-Eleven in my neighborhood? I must secure nectar of the cow lest my queen be disappointed, and so I have brought much silver and gold and colorful beads to appease the keeper of the Slim Jims behind the counter, who appears to be in a wretched mood when I beseech him to avert his gaze from the renderings of breasts in the stroke-scroll unfurled before him and come forth to tally my meager purchase.

Okay, maybe I'm a little rebellious when it comes to the whole technological blitzkrieg. Nothing serious. I'm not going to stop shaving and live in a dirt-floored Fotomat in Quiet Lonerville, Montana, because I hallucinated that the Keno board at the Desert Inn was mocking me. You know, it's just that everywhere I look, there's such a dependence on synthetic forms of communication.

Whatever happened to good old-fashioned face-to-face insincerity?

As for my computer skills, you know there hasn't been anyone that ineffective at a keyboard since Susan Dey was in *The Partridge Family*.

Computers now control every aspect of our lives, and in fact this stuff I'm telling you right now is on a computer. And yes, I too am a computer: the Dennistron 2000. The real Dennis is in a Rand Corporation building locked away for his own good with an electrode attached to his brain and a cord leading up to a pleasure button he bangs away at like a little toy monkey with a brass cymbal. And you know what? Dennis is happy.

If you don't know how to use a computer, like me, one day, and that day is very soon, you are going to find yourself at the complete mercy of your children. Because while you've been blustering and bumbling through the computer age with all the technical proficiency of Tennessee Tuxedo's assistant Chumley, your Mr. Whoopee-like seven-year-old can reroute the space shuttle to land on the 405, crash the Belgian stock market, and convince complete strangers to donate their balls to a comet. When it comes to computers, your kids are MacGyver and you are a Hasidic Amish guy. And when your complete lack of computer knowledge becomes painfully obvious to your children, they will take the same condescending tone with you that Alex Trebek takes when he corrects somebody on *Jeopardy!* "Oh, I'm sorry, Dad. The correct answer was 'the on-off switch.' 'That's the on-off switch.' Mom, you were the last correct questioner, please select again."

Now, as for the Internet, it is an amazing communications tool that's bringing the whole world together. I mean, you sit down to sign on to America Online in your hometown, and it's just staggering to think that at the same moment, halfway around the world in China, someone you've never met is sitting at their computer, hearing the exact same busy signal that you're hearing.

Now, as for me, I think computers will remain a fogbound protuberance around which I'll navigate the rest of my life. I'll keep my eye on them and do my best to avoid them. Besides, if I ever feel the need to access artificial intelligence, I'll just watch celebrity week on *Wheel of Fortune,* okay? And, you know, it'll save me from having to learn all those new terms. *Ram* will still be McCartney's last good album. . . . A hard drive will remain a trip to your in-laws. . . . And you know what? I'll always harken back to a time when clicking your mouse too much could make you go blind.

The World Wide Web we weave is a tangled one, my friends. For the time being, I believe I'll let my kids play their computer games, but I also think, for the time being, the only Web they'll be accessing is Charlotte's. And how do you keep the kids away from the Internet? Two words. *Mandatory television.*

Of course, that's just my opinion, I could be wrong.

Mothers

A sixty-three-year-old woman has had a baby last year. You know what the first clue was she was pregnant? She missed her Jurassic Period.

Now, I don't want to get off on a rant here, but with the second Sunday in May looming over our conscience like a guilt-radiating mushroom cloud, I would like to take a few moments off from my weekly turn as Mr. Curmudgeonly McCranky to thank those tireless nurturers who, for better or worse, have formed us into who we are today. I'm talking about the woman who changed your diapers, kissed your boo-boos, sat up all night with you when you were sick, disapproved of your friends, and caught you masturbating so many times that eventually you couldn't get off until she busted through the door. I'm talking about your mom.

The mother-child relationship has always been a complex one, fraught with more ambivalence and emotional misfires than Martin Lawrence and Amanda Plummer touring in *The Gin Game*.

Unshakable bastions of well-meaning dysfunction, mothers somehow teach us about the world while protecting us from its dangers, encourage us to be independent while carefully rationing our freedom, and manage to instill in us the belief that we're the best while simultaneously making us feel like we're never good enough. Only a mother possesses the unique ability to envelop you in a soft, warm blanket of unconditional love at the exact same moment that she's driving you *fucking crazy*.

When you're a kid, basically your mother's job is to make you look like a dork. The mittens pinned to your jacket, the Elmer Fudd earflap hat, the rubber boots with the Wonder bread bags over your feet, and of course the pièce de résistance, the snow pants. There's an outfit that just screams "Beat the shit out of me and take my lunch money."

And why did Mom insist on cutting my hair herself until I was fourteen? She had a home haircut kit that looked like Mengele's briefcase and the barber skills of Dr. Leatherface brandishing a flowbee. All right. She'd finish and say "Well, how does that look?" I'd say, "Yeah. Looks good, Mom" because in case my school does a stage production of *Sling Blade,* this haircut makes me look like Karl's stupider friend who couldn't get laid with Brad Pitt's dick. All right." Now, where's my snow pants, I have to ride that girl's bike you bought me past the tough kids to my piano lesson.

Then, at night, she'd make it all better when she'd tuck me in, kiss me on the forehead, and say, "Now, I don't want to get off on a rant here, but once upon a time, there were three little pigs."

But as you get older, you realize that mothers also have the ability to get under your skin faster than a splinter on a waterslide. When you're a teenager, having your mother take your messages is like hiring a heroin addict to do your taxes. Your messages are always going to be garbled, like "Jenooga called and said the mall can't be bitten." Okay. Thanks, Mom. I'll get the code breakers on that.

You know you can put up a front in the real world, but your mom sees through that faster than Superman sees through Lois Lane's pants suit. Mothers can work a thirty-years-gone umbilical cord like Zorro lighting matches with a whip. And since she's got the psychological and emotional drop on you, your mom pushes buttons like a peyote dealer working straight commission.

And you know what, a mother's claim on your psyche is wholly substantiated because you love her so much. And the reason you love her so much is that she was your arrival terminal. She created you, so you always owe her and can never really repay the debt. Being born is like asking Don Corleone for a favor.

There's a very good explanation for why cult leaders force members to cut off all contact with their families. Because they know that their spell will be broken and all the mind control will disappear the instant you hear your mother saying: "And I suppose that just because your new friends are having themselves castrated so they can go on the spaceship, you have to do it too, right?"

The relationship between mothers and children never changes, and that's because no matter how rich or powerful you are, your mother still remembers when you were three and put SpaghettiOs up your nose.

Even if you're the guy who signs Alan Greenspan's paychecks, your mom has either cleaned or stuck a thermometer in every single orifice of your body. So if you're a bazillionaire captain of industry or a Nobel Prize winner, your mom may be proud, but she's not impressed. She would be a lot more impressed if you'd stand up straight, chew your food, clean up your room, marry that nice Jenkins girl, and for God's sakes, quit masturbating and pull up your snow pants. Now.

Of course, that's just my opinion, I could be wrong.

Immigration

Now, I don't want to get off on a rant here, but is America still the melting pot? Or has it become a crock?

The thing that made our country unique and remarkable was its open-armed willingness to accept all people who needed refuge from their dysfunctional mother- and fatherlands. That's what America has always been, a teen shelter for runaways from abusive families.

But the simple era of immigration is long over. Right now in this country, immigration is looked on about as fondly as Billy Ray Cyrus opening for Trent Reznor. Once the world's biggest, friendliest open house, America now has all the grace and sensitivity of a New York City co-op board interviewing Martin Lawrence.

Now, one reason for this is that by the year 2050 there may be 400 million Americans, and 320 million of them will be in *my* way on the fucking 405 freeway.

Now, I'm by no means a xenophobe, but our borders are being violated more often than Courtney Love in a mosh-pit at the Citadel.

Sure, people complain about illegal aliens, but they don't complain about getting the cheap immigrant labor they provide. At least I'm up front about it. Every morning on my way into work I drive by the Writers Guild and there's usually twenty or twenty-five Mexican comedy writers hanging around the sidewalk, waiting for work. You know—I'll pick a few of them up. *Viva referencia obscura!*

Now, not only do people complain about illegal aliens, they complain about all foreigners. But you know what you have to admit about foreigners? They're funny. They do things in an odd way; they have strange customs, and they talk weird. And often when you laugh at them they don't understand what's going on and they laugh right along with you.

Immigrants supply us with many things, not the least of which is a defenseless target and scapegoat, an invaluable commodity in the eternally bullish markets of politics and blame.

Look, we're all just people who happen to live in this place called America. At one time we thought that this land went on forever and ever with nothing but space and fruit-laden trees ahead. But just the way when you were a child and your bedroom looked so enormous and then years later you were confounded by how you ever fitted into that tiny bed, our perspective as a nation has to change and grow up too. It's pathetic that the Viper Room has better security at the door than we do at our borders.

We have to do something, we have to do something to stop *illegal* immigration. It threatens not only us but the legal immigrants too. Our border police are basically mall cops with night goggles on, okay? They just keep hiring more and more agents for the U.S. Border Patrol, and although the situation on the Mexican border is still not under control, I'm happy to report that we have things on the Canadian border pretty much well in hand. Oh, sure, the occasional crafty Canadian will slip through dressed as a giant beaver, but that's the exception. For the most part, we've beaten down the Canucks to the point where they're resigned to just stay home and think of new animals to put on their currency.

Listen, immigrants who come to this country looking for a free ride should be asked to leave. But I also believe that third- and fourth-generation Americans, those whose papers are perfectly in order but whose lives aren't, should also be told to leave. In fact, let's ship the whole country to Greenland and start bringing everyone back in here on a case-by-case basis. In the meantime, here are some guidelines for newcomers to our hallowed, syringe-laden shores.

1. I don't care how they wait on line in your country. Stop fucking pushing me, okay?

2. Pets of immigrants have to be able to do tricks. One thing this country does not need is any more unskilled dogs.

Dennis Miller

3. You leave those little nut-hugger swimsuits over on the coisette, okay. Yeah, you leave those over at Cannes, okay, Baron Von Hard-on?

4. If you're a local news anchor from a Latino background, congratulations. I applaud your success in a competitive field. Now, do you think you can read the news without turning into Che Guevara hitting on Evita Peron at a Cinco de Mayo dance when it comes time to pronounce the words "Costa Rica"?

And finally, at least learn to swear in English. I don't want to be flipped off again by some guy telling me to go fack myself.

Of course, that's just my opinion, I could be wrong.

Bad Habits

Now, I don't want to get off on a rant here, but we as a nation have more bad habits than a moth-infested nunnery.

We are a nation of elastic-waistbanded, television-glued, crack-smoking, pork-rind-stuffing, natural-resource-hogging fat-asses, aren't we, folks? Why is that? How come the French wallow in cigarettes and goose fat, drink a supertanker of wine per person at lunch, yet have so much less alcoholism, heart disease, and obesity than we do? Well, unless there's an undiscovered link between bathing and hardening of the arteries, I'd have to venture a guess that a lot of it has to do with mental attitude.

America was founded by Puritans, and like it or not, the antipleasure dogma of those buckle-shoed killjoys still pervades our collective unconscious like an IMAX shot of Dennis Franz's naked, hairy cop ass. Hence, anything enjoyable is automatically forbidden and bad, and in our panic to avoid it at all costs, we become obsessed with it. Like dressing up in a pink teddy and a pair of Ugg boots and repeatedly screaming the word *"verboten"* into a conch shell balanced on the back of a miniature pony. Oh, I see. That would just be me, right?

One characteristic that appears to be uniquely American is our complete lack of understanding of the word *moderation.* Is it any wonder that the same culture that came up with the all-you-can-eat dessert bar also spawned more 12-step programs than a line-dancing jury?

We share an all-or-nothing mentality that creates an insatiable market for supersized fast-food meals, double-crust double-stuffed deep-dish pizzas and dirigible-sized cinnabuns, plus gas-guzzling Winnebagos to drive the two fucking blocks to get all of these items. Then we look at ourselves in a full-length mirror and think: "Wow, how odd. That sea-sow is not only walking on dry land, but is wearing exactly the same outfit that I am." We then go on Slim-Fast and Jenny Craig and subject ourselves to the kind of deprivation that a penitent Buddhist monk would find gratuitous. Deprivation, of course, ultimately produces craving, and we're right back at square one on the crash-and-burn game board.

Of course, human beings do not have a patent on self-destructive behavior; it shows up in nature all the time. The lemming that's drawn to the cliff, the salmon that kills itself trying to swim upstream, and, of course, the chimpanzee that rides the miniature bicycle without wearing a helmet.

Let's put some of America's bad habits under the microscope. New evidence is showing that cigarette manufacturers may have deliberately manipulated amounts of nicotine to make them even more addictive. Cigarettes with varying degrees of nicotine makes sense. Lights, for times when you're just out with friends having some shits and giggles. Mediums, for unexpected bills and family disagreements. Heavy, for when Dennis Rodman comes to pick up your daughter. And extra-heavy for when Dennis Rodman comes to pick up your son.

One spiral out from smoking on the vice schematic are drugs. Now, I know that certain cultures use drugs to commune with the spirits of animal guardians and tap the wisdom of the elders who've gone before them—but not us, no no, not us. We use drugs in much the same way a dog licks its own balls. It feels good as long as you don't stop to think about what you're actually doing. I was going to say "a dog's ass" but I changed it because this is a family book. Dog balls, something the whole family can enjoy.

And finally, America's most insidious and most pervasive vice, our eating habits. We buy our hamburgers by the pound, our chicken by the bucket, and our pizza by the foot.

You've got bad eating habits if you use a grocery cart in 7-Eleven, okay?

Now, I tend to think that bad habits are an inevitable side effect of prosperity. Only when a person's waking hours aren't devoted to finding food, clothing, and shelter can there be time for extraneous activities like picking your nose and gambling. And the more you have, the more you want, and since we here in America are lucky/cursed to have the most, our need for a jolt escalates exponentially with each passing generation.

This explains why every year, the Six Flags amusement park unveils yet another ride designed for one reason and one reason only: to make me shit my pants and shame myself in front of my children. As a matter of fact, I understand that now Six Flags is working on a ride where you're elevated to 150 feet and then dropped head-first onto a slab of concrete. And you just know that some Beaver Knievel kid is gonna complain that there were no poisoned spikes embedded into the cement.

As a culture, we're trapped in a vicious cycle where we are so benumbed by a constant barrage of stimuli, the only thing that registers with us is more, bigger, better, louder stimuli. Tired of pot? Try cocaine. Tired of cocaine? Try crack. Tired of crack? Try driving cross country with Kramer and the guy from *Shine*.

Of course, that's just my opinion, I could be wrong.

Lawyers

You know, there's an old joke that goes "What do you call a hundred lawyers at the bottom of the ocean?" and the answer is "A good start." Uh . . . well, no, it isn't a good start. Because you put a hundred lawyers on the bottom of the ocean and pretty soon every single fish and crustacean will be talked into a class action suit naming Mrs. Paul, Arthur Treacher, and the fucking Gorton's fisherman as defendants.

Now, I don't want to get off on a rant here, but our country's once-venerable justice system has been taken over by a pack of grotesquely rapacious truth-pimps who, in the interest of lining their own custom-tailored Armani pockets, are more tort happy than Pavarotti turned loose in an Entenmann's factory.

Okay, I'll grant you that there are still lawyers out there who are motivated by compassion and concern, lawyers like our guest tonight, Counselor Bugliosi, but they're about as easy to find as a dry spot on Billy Idol's futon.

I'm talking about the lawyers who are paid huge fees to represent the most despicable people in the world— like drug dealers, O. J. Simpson, child molesters, rapists, O. J. Simpson, O. J. Simpson, and O. J. Simpson.

We've all heard about the burglar who trips and falls while leaving the scene of the crime and then sues the guy whose house he broke into, or the woman who spills hot coffee on herself and sues the restaurant for serving it to her, or the moron college student who falls out of the window while mooning some of his friends and then sues the school.

The reason that virtually any product in this country is ten times more expensive than it should be is that for every marble brain that either eats a silicon packet or decides to make toast in the bathtub, it becomes Sadie Hawkins Day for squadrons of ambulance-chasing legalistas peeling off from the main formation to bomb the shit out of our economy with no regard for the collateral damage they might wreak.

It wasn't always this way. The word "lawyer" used to conjure up images of an upstanding, tireless advocate for the little guy. An Atticus Finch or Clarence Darrow, who was passionately dedicated to truth and justice. Lawyers were once regarded with respect bordering on reverence; now they're viewed with about the same amount of enthusiasm as Matt Helm at a radical feminist poetry reading.

Like Pamela Anderson Lee, the legal profession started out with good intentions, just somewhere along the line it got really scary.

Why the change? Why the change? When did the field of law attain the status of a pork chop at the Western Wall?

Well, the truth, the whole truth, and nothing but the truth is that the law has been bastardized by a band of hucksters who have made it so cryptic, so utterly puzzling and arcane that even Moses, Hammurabi, and Judge Judy working around the clock for twenty years could not understand it. Modern American lawyers employ English not spoken since the days of King George the Third and Latin that even Gloria Estefan couldn't grasp, all right, purposely making it impossible for even the wisest layman to interpret the true meaning of the law. We have gone from Thou shalt not kill to Thou shalt not deprive any or all persons of their inalienable right to absorb or dispense hereforth with any or all oxygen delivery and removal systems contained within or near said living configuration.

It is often said that while our legal system is a flawed one, it's still the best in the world. Well, you know something? I think we're being a bit too easy on ourselves. I happen to think the American legal system sucks worse than a Celine Dion cover version of "Whole Lotta Love." You know it, and I know it. Americans walking into a courtroom have long abandoned any expectation of justice. Because the American legal system has been turned into nothing more than a baroque multitiered Vulcan chess game where the rules have become too intricate for the average citizen to play and where the loser is no longer the guilty party but rather the least clever of the two. Lack of wit shouldn't be a crime—unless of course you're Andy Rooney. . . . "You ever notice I'm dead? Why is that?"

Most lawyers care about justice and what is right as much as MTV viewers care about Jenny McCarthy's weltanschauung. No, no, I think you misinterpreted that. Weltanschauung is a German word for her world view. Her tits are hootershnapples.

People ask, How can a lawyer deem himself or herself to be simultaneously an ethical person and a defender of pure evil? How can anyone stand before a jury knowing full well in his heart that the person they are defending is guilty? Well, the answer is very simple. Lawyers who defend scum are, in their minds, defending something more important than the person sitting to their left. They are defending the law of our land. And that's what we have to change.

We have to change the idea that the lawyer can use the Bill of Rights as a pillow every night and sleep soundly because he feels in his heart even though he has defended subhumans and gotten them off he is just doing what is constitutionally dictated. We have to put the onus back on the lawyer as an individual. The lawyer must take responsibility for his actions. We make it too easy on them when we attach patriotism to handling animals like Lyle and Erik Menendez.

And while we're talking about injustice in the world, how come Lyle always gets mentioned first? Lyle and Erik. Lyle and Erik. Lyle and Erik. I mean, come on, it's not even alphabetical. You know what I think? I think

Erik should sue Lyle's ass. That is, if the other inmates can just stop cross-examining it for a few minutes.

William Shakespeare once said, "The first thing we do is kill all the lawyers." Of course, he said that after he lost all of his sonnets in a nasty division of property settlement when he divorced Lady Anna Nicole of Smith. Well, obviously, no one's advocating that we kill all the lawyers. But it is time that we tighten the choke chain and make these attack dogs more accountable. I say we make law school four years—the last year spent learning how to vaguely resemble a human being. And most important, if you get a bad guy off through a sleazy loophole, he bunks with you.

Of course, that's just my opinion, I could be wrong.

Fashion

Boy, imagine being an actress. You go to acting classes, you participate in some spectacularly embarrassing scene work with some kid from Hermosa Beach named Chaz, who's presently valet-parking at Tommy Tang's but who eventually wants to do a one-man salute to Liv Ullmann at halftime of the Clipper games, you finally break through Hollywood's notorious glass ceiling, you get nominated for the highest award your craft can bestow, but if you wear the wrong color gown, you got Joan Rivers's kid sticking her finger down her throat after you walk through the fucking press line. You know, Joan Rivers telling Lauren Bacall her dress is all wrong is like Carrot Top telling Lenny Bruce he needs to get an edge.

Now, I don't want to get off on a rant here, but at this point fashion has been declared dead more times than a narcoleptic Jason Voorhees. Yet every season it manages to resurrect itself one more time to lurch down the runway in all of its irrelevant splendor.

People have been obsessed with fashion ever since the Garden of Eden when Eve said to Adam, "You know, that fig leaf you have on is so last season."

Fashion is the way humans provide what nature didn't. It's our plumage, our fur, our scales. The number-one reason people like to look good is to attract a mate. Now, since Our Maker, who by the way designs for the House of God, did not provide us with fancy tail feathers or a bulging throat sac, or that weird red thing that hangs out of a baboon's ass—since he didn't provide us with any of those, we wear clothing.

During prehistoric times everyone wore the same thing every day. I mean, look at Wilma Flintstone. She's always sporting the same tight, short skirt with that shredded zigzag cut three inches above her knee. Oh, you know she knew she had a nice pair of gams there, she wasn't afraid to let you know. Thighs like a vise. So what's she doing staying home and just raising the family? You know she was frustrated. Someone like Wilma needed more. And there's Fred, stuffing his fat fuck-face, not giving her the attention she needed, and, might I add, deserved. Yeah, while you were busy fantasizing about Ginger, or Marsha Brady, I spotted the woman who really needed it. Needed it from me. Wilma. And maybe Betty would walk in on us and let out that nervous giggle when she saw my massive thickasaurus and kazoos hovering over us with the prehistoric Martian equivalent of a camcorder, making a sick, Paleolithic Bob Crane film that he can take back to his home planet for parties and such. Oh, yeah, that's what I want. Oh, where was I . . .

Now, the problem here is that I don't have a clue as to the meaning of contemporary fashion. In fact, I thought prêt-à-porter was where French construction workers went to the bathroom. But it appears to me that the fashion industry preys on our diametrically opposed needs to be different while at the same time fitting in.

Fashion is commerce built on envy. Know why fashion magazines are always thicker than the Tokyo Donnelly directory? Because they're full of ads that are trying to make you think that if you use this raspberry/kiwi/placenta thigh cream, your life is going to change, and articles that are trying to make you believe that if you wear this Dolce & Gabbana dress, you're gonna look just like the ninety-five-pound heroin addict who's modeling it.

I mean, fashion is brilliant from the seller's point of view: They tell you this is what you must buy to fit in, to be one of the "in" people. Then, a few months later, they tell you what you bought is now out, and you're an asshole, you're uncool, and now you have to buy this to fit in. The fashion industry, like the cigarette industry, actually creates both the supply and the demand.

Now, men seem less susceptible to this sort of arrogance. And I'm not sure whether we're more insightful or just more oblivious when it comes to fashion. Yes, I *am* sure. We're more oblivious. As far as fashion is concerned, we are more out of it than Strom Thurmond on a little brown jug of NyQuil. Okay? As we all know, originally men's clothing served only two purposes: Sure, to keep us warm. But first and foremost clothes were invented to prevent women from seeing how small our penises were during the winter.

If there is indeed a bottom line to this Möbius strip of parading clowns, it is to just slow down a little and look at yourself for a second. Here are some basic rules for fashion:

1. When considering whether or not to have a metal stud put through your tongue, or your belly button or your genitalia, take lightning into account.

2. Never wear a Budweiser cap with a Coors T-shirt. Commit.

3. Hey, Levi Strauss. 501's? 505's? 509's? What am I, buying pants or catching a fucking train?

4. If you walk around a mall with your baseball cap on backward, you better be black or a catcher.

5. If you're going to murder your ex-wife and her male companion, don't wear incredibly rare designer shoes.

6. When using a Magic Marker to color in your ankle to cover a hole in your socks, make sure the Magic Marker color matches the socks.

And finally, men, if you have tits, don't walk around in a tight T-shirt. It confuses the children.

Folks, fashion, this clever marketing ruse in the guise of cloaking oneself against the elements, has gone on long enough. Fashion is becoming, quite frankly, unfashionable, and it's time to stop allowing yourselves to be bullied by the whims of some out-of-touch, chain-smoking European drip whose only friend is Elsa Klensch. But I do understand the need to be chic, the need to be au courant, the need to make a statement, so let me offer my solution.

I say we put heterosexual men in charge of fashion. Ladies, you'll never need to read *Vogue* magazine or do a wardrobe overhaul again. If we're in charge, here's the only outfit you'll ever need: miniskirt, high heels, midriff. Evening wear? Fishnet stockings and French-cut panties. Trust me, darlings, you'll be *fabulous*.

Of course, that's just my opinion, I could be wrong.

Bad TV

As with any other recreational drug, television, when used judiciously, can be a pleasant experience. I know I'm gonna get death threats from William Bennett for saying this, but TV is responsible for a lot of spontaneous education. How many times have you been channel surfing, when suddenly you click onto a special on the Discovery channel about giant squids fucking and for the next hour you're completely spellbound and oddly stimulated?

But I'm not talking about good television. The topic here is bad television and America's insatiable thirst for it. It's easy to figure out. We all work hard during the day and TV is our main source of entertainment. Did you hear me? Entertainment. Most people don't watch TV for enlightenment, they just want a giggle as they doze off.

Now, I don't want to get off on a rant here, but America's jones for bad TV is growing faster than your penis while watching that squid thing I mentioned earlier.

Television is the most important invention since the wheel, and I might add most of us first learned about the wheel from television. Every night millions of Americans Krazy Glue down the scan button on their clickers and strobe past great, great stuff like HBO's *Larry Sanders,* HBO's *Tracey Takes On,* HBO's *Tales from the Crypt,* HBO's *Dream On,* and HBO's original movies to settle in to an evening of albinos wrestling in a steel cage.

You know, a man can work up a powerful lip parch kissing that much ass.

TV is the great equalizer. Bill Clinton may be making decisions on our nation's security during the day, but at night he is laughing his ass off at some guy getting hit in the nuts with a rake on *America's Funniest Home Videos.*

To assure that everyone's going to "get it," the three major networks have to make certain their programs are about as challenging as bowling during a 7.4 on the Richter scale. Their job is to make sure that the only thing that goes over our collective heads is the hat that holds two beer cans with the Styrofoam tits on the front. Thus, they give us shows that are blander than Strom Thurmond's diet.

And any show that doesn't pull numbers like a bingo caller on methamphetamines is immediately snuffed.

A perfect example of how imperfect the TV rating system is is the fact that a few years ago the show

M.A.N.T.I.S. was taken off the air. One of the greatest shows ever, it was about a guy that was half man, half praying mantis, and he fought crime. And they cancel it! A regular guy who, when trouble reared its ugly head, half of him would turn into a praying mantis!

Don't you see the beauty of that, for chrissakes? Why didn't any of you fuckers watch . . . why? Sorry, but I guess there's a little mantis inside all of us. Manty, we hardly knew ye.

It's true, everybody watches bad TV. Now they are talking about five hundred channels. I can't wait to see what kind of brilliantly horrific programs are out there when we get up to half a thou. Hey, I'd give the "cat box" channel a chance if it came with basic cable.

And the cat box channel would be only one short step in front of daytime talk shows on the dolt meter.

If there's one thing that these shows have done, it's given overweight, big-haired southern women a forum in which to air their grievances.

Yeah. Let's face it, what are the chances that Ted Koppel is going to devote a half hour to helping fifteen-year-old Kimmy understand why her twenty-seven-year-old mother, Kimmy Senior, will date only Jamaican Siamese twins?

Here is the single most noticeable phenomenon of daytime talk shows: unbelievably grotesque men, men where you can literally see the dog-shit fumes coming off their hair, surrounded by two somewhat attractive women who don't mind sharing him.

Dennis Miller

The entire multibillion-dollar industry of daytime talk shows is predicated upon one simple subtext: I can't believe anybody is actually fucking that person.

And then there're the game shows. I always derive a cathartic moment when I watch a Chicklet-lobed Moorlock on *Wheel of Fortune* who opts to buy an "O" when the puzzle topic is body of water and the puzzle reads M blank S-S blank S-S blank P-P blank. Look, there's a reason *Wheel of Fortune* is on right after *Jeopardy!* Once you've been forced to choke down the foul-tasting tequila shot of your own abject ignorance, it's nice to be able to bite into the refreshing lime wedge of other people's incredible fucking stupidity.

Listen, bad television is three things. A bullet train to a morally bankrupt youth. A slow spiral into an intellectual void. And, of course, a complete blast to watch.

Much as bad TV may remind us of a terrible accident that you just can't look away from, there's nothing accidental about its badness.

Unctuous hosts, nonexistent production values, freakazoid guests, drekky theme music . . . all serve a complex, calculated purpose: They feed our dark and covert need to feel superior to others.

Folks, we can point fingers all we want, but it's the finger pushing the button on the remote control that is calling the shots. Face it, we are moths, and bad television is the porch light we've been slamming our heads against for decades now.

Not because it affords any illumination but because it barely beats eating socks.

Bad TV is part of our culture and harmless enough when properly abused. You know what? I say we should push it even further and wring the bad TV chamois for every last drop of stupid juice it contains.

Am I the only one who thinks they should put a laugh track on the show *Cops?* How's about shoplifter's week on *Supermarket Sweep?* What about Susan Powter as Sergeant Carter in the *Gomer Pyle* remake? How's about O.J. and Kathie Lee? Huh? Let's sew a tiny third arm onto Richard Bey's forehead. And finally, what about *un*willing contestants on *American Gladiators?* Turbo, Laser, I believe you know Mr. Limbaugh.

Of course that's just my opinion, I could be wrong.

Feminism

Ah, feminism in the nineties, what a "what is yours what is mine field."

Now, I don't want to get off on a rant here, but the feminist movement of the nineties is going off in more directions than Don King's hair in an electrical storm. You know, to be an überfrau in the nineties is to be as confused as Al D'Amato on Celebrity *Jeopardy!* Current-day feminists are slapped with more labels than a telephone pole in front of a coffeehouse at Wellesley and draw more enmity than Linda McCartney at a Tony Roma's. You know, they're stereotypically portrayed as humorless, multiple-cat-owning viragos wearing shapeless home-tie-dyed dresses and Karloffing around in Doc Martens while hosting their own public-access cable shows called the *No-Fly Zone.*

Which is unfair because despite the Janet Reno–sized strides over the past twenty years, there are still gender inequities in our society that are more glaring than a freshly buffed diamond tiara on the Bonneville Salt Flats at high noon.

Having drinks bought for you and being able to cry your way out of a speeding ticket don't make up for lower wages, date rape, pickup trucks with naked women silhouetted on the mud flaps, no affordable child care, happy-handed bosses, not being called on in class even when you know the answer, and having to take most of the responsibility for birth control. Recently, we're seeing women's rights violated in places as disparate as a condo in Brentwood, California, and a Mitsubishi plant in Normal, Illinois. Hey, listen, everyone's got a right to work at their job without being bullied and humiliated.

And as long as there are people out there who are so threatened, so consumed with hatred and fear that they have to use what little power they have to take those rights away from women, you can bet your sensible boots there's gonna be a feminist movement.

And there will always be men who are threatened by that movement. Feminism in the nineties has left in its wake a gaggle of men more flustered than Les Nessman reporting live from the MTV Malibu beach house.

And no man is more threatened than Rush Limbaugh, who is the quintessential male antifeminist. Now, anybody who hasn't even seen his own penis in the past ten years is bound to be antiwoman.

Dennis Miller

But while it has been slow in coming, men *are*, they finally are in the process of divesting themselves of much of their undeserved and unwarranted power. Guys, we had to give it up. It was time to share the power because we were ruining everything. For the survival of our species and our planet, evolution reclaimed our crown and made us share it, because, quite frankly, leaving the planet Earth in the hands of only men is like asking Moe Howard to baby-sit a colicky infant.

Anyway, while I agree with the majority of the feminists' causes and I admire their passion and commitment, oftentimes their approach leaves much to be desired.

But before the earth goddess SWAT team comes and takes me away to the Reprogramming Camp for the Estrogen Impaired, where I'll learn to become a more nurturing, sensitive man with a developed feminine side who can bake bread and then perform foreplay for five hours at a pop . . . before that happens, may I put forth the following suggestions. . . .

One. If you want your message heard, leave the rage to Alanis Morrisette, okay? Because when you're strident, you remind us of our moms yelling at us and we do to you what we did to them . . . we ignore you.

Number two—opposed as I am to violence against women, would somebody ask Oddjob to please take Camille Paglia and her leopard-trimmed Humvee out to the junkyard and place them in the compactor?

And three. Sisters, let's be more inclusive of different approaches. Many of today's younger women have become alienated from the feminist movement because of the extreme messages being sent by its more vociferous leaders. No one likes to be told they're a traitor because they quit their job to stay home with a baby or like to wear high heels and makeup. You can't spend every nanosecond of your life trying to elevate the gender. There has to be room for compromise, for allowing for differences between women. We need to respect Shannon Faulkner and Shannon Tweed.

Now, look, I'm not trying to sell you a carton of Virginia Slims here. But listen to me: Yes, women still find doors shut tighter than a Jehovah's Witness approaching Mark Fuhrman's house.

And, yes, most corporate headquarters have more glass ceilings than Carl Sagan's town house. But for women to fixate only on what they haven't accomplished without stepping back to marvel at how quickly and far they have advanced in the past twenty years is going to make them feel more fucked over than lining up for two hours to see a taping of *Mike and Maty* only to discover that Maty's been sidelined by the flu.

You know what I want? I want to live in a world where women are allowed to fail as badly as men and then get a better job and a raise just like men. And I'm hoping that you'll remember that I said that, and I was always on your side, 'cause I don't want to be hurt in the coming revolution. And by the way, don't you all look sexy in your little uniforms.

Of course, that's just my wife's opinion, I could be wrong.

Dennis Miller

Washington, D.C.

Ah, Washington, D.C. Now, I don't want to get off on a rant here, but it's more obvious than Marlon Brando in a Day-Glo thong that our nation's capital runs on the kind of you-scratch-my-back-and-I'll-scratch-yours mentality that one rarely sees outside of Ed Asner in a burlap tube top.

The stories of corruption that manage to leak their way out of Washington barely hint at the degree of venality, the positively Byzantine intrigue, that fuels day-to-day doings along the Potomac. Special-interest groups, PACs, lobbies . . . there's more palms being greased on any given day in D.C. than there are in a boys' dorm during MTV's *The Grind*. You know, if

Frank Capra took a look at today's Washington, Mr. Smith would have stayed home. Let's face it, our nation's capital is more self-serving than Ikea, and our lawmakers get more perks than Jerry Lewis in the twenty-third hour of the fucking telethon.

Washington, D.C., is no longer an honored and revered institution commanding the respect of its republic, but a soap opera circus, a tabloid dart board, a Hollywood with better acting, a bemusement park called Punditland, where the rides are four years long and the popcorn is a billion dollars for a small bucket.

Washington was built on a bog. And in a scant two hundred years it has grown from a dirty swamp into a bureaucratic quagmire. At one time Washington actually meant something. But now it's about as relevant as Bob Dylan's tuning fork.

The main problem with Marion Barry's District of Colombian is that it just . . . it seems like nothing ever gets done there. It's like an Etch-A-Sketch that gets shaken every fourth November, just never hard enough to completely erase that residual maze of dangling connections and stairs to nowhere.

The average American works about three hours each day to pay taxes to keep Washington, D.C., humming. Go to Washington and see what that gets you. You won't see that much cash being pissed away at Vitamin Expo '98.

Washington is clubbier than an LAPD-sponsored baby seal hunt and more insular than the Freemen compound under quarantine for the Andromeda strain. It's a system in which the demands of survival cancel out the

Dennis Miller

qualities one would expect in a public servant, like intelligence, integrity, and selflessness. Instead, those who are most successful in public office have got a jones for power and influence that makes *Naked Lunch* read like *The Velveteen Rabbit*. It's the only town where the phenomenally untalented, boorish, and downright stupid can Quayle their way up the ladder and into the national spotlight.

Al D'Amato . . . Al D'Amato? I mean, did the entire state of New York get drunk one day and elect him just for a goof? Al D'Amato is a waste of an apostrophe. Allowing this guy to chair an ethics committee is like having Kevorkian teach you the Heimlich maneuver.

Newt Gingrich? Newt Gingrich is so cold, when he opens his mouth a light goes on. This guy's further to the right than the part in Sam Donaldson's hair.

Strom Thurmond's birthday cake has more candles than a Sting video. This guy used to baby-sit Bob Dole, for chrissake.

You know, folks, some are born great, others achieve greatness, and still others have greatness thrust upon them. And then there's Washington, D.C. There, a good man is harder to find than Montel Williams's cowlick.

We're talking about a group of people who wouldn't know greatness unless it donated a large sum of money to their reelection campaign and asked for only a small favor in return.

But maybe there's some light at the end of the reflecting pool. Voters are getting tired of the name-calling and back-biting that goes on in politics. There's more labeling going on on Capitol Hill than in a Wal-Mart the night before the Labor Day weekend. Political philosophies and platforms are now quartered into inside or outside, left or right. It's like we're calling pitches. Clinton, to the left and inside, Dole to the right and inside. Ross Perot? High and outside. Buchanan? Hit the fucking batter.

It's time to get past the labels and check the contents within the package, that in many cases has settled all too comfortably at the bottom of the legislative bag.

Look, if our nation's capital is a monster, we're not only the angry, torch-carrying taxpayers looking to cut its head off, we're also Dr. Frankenvoter. We went into the booth that stormy night, we pulled the lever, and screamed, "It's alive." Well, guess what, pal? It is, and it's incumbent upon us to realize that ultimately we're the Hazelwood on this D. C. Valdez, and if we keep trying to sleep through our shifts and letting the other guy steer, we're going to end up on the rocks spewing wasted democracy.

The solution is very simple. Move election day to April 15. Pay your taxes and hold elections on the same day. See if any of these duplicitous sons of bitches would try to get away with their crap if we paid their salaries on the same day as we voted for them. I don't think so. Storm the Bastille.

Let us eat cake and let them eat me. Of course, that's just my opinion, I could be wrong.

The Royal Family

The Kennedys are the closest thing we have to a royal family. What is this morbid fascination we have with the concept of someone automatically *born* to be better than we are? Leave it to us to sail away from England's tyrannical rule, only to be completely fixated on the royals.

Now, I don't want to get off on a rant here, but for a country that regards Americans in approximately the same light as Murray held Ted Baxter, the comportment of England's royal family these last few years would probably get them banned from Billy Idol's tour bus. Much like major league baseball, the throne of England has deteriorated from its grand and glorious past into an infighting, badly behaved, exorbitantly expensive institution that nobody can really remember the point of anymore.

At one time in history, it made perfect sense that a country's leaders should have absolute power and reign over their subjects as God's proxy. And, at one time, burning witches and dying of smallpox made perfect sense too. Come on, everybody knows that the concept of the divine right of monarchs is nearly as dated as the outfits on the roller-disco episode of *CHiPs*. And yet the English accept without question the pomp and circumstance that accompany the crown, even though at this point in time it all seems to have about as much meaning as a collection of feminist essays by Anna Nicole Smith. Sure, you hear some discontented Johnny Rotten rumbling from time to time, but for all intents and purposes the British monarchy is as entrenched as Rush Limbaugh in a hammock.

You know, in a modern world, what purpose do these members of the unbelievably lucky-sperm club serve other than to make jug-eared, needle-nosed commoners feel better about their looks? My God, the royal families of Europe have been inbreeding for so long, their genealogy chart has fewer branches on it than Charlie Brown's Christmas tree.

The current-day role of the queen is as a hood ornament in a bad hat, an overpaid plaster-of-Paris deep-sea diver at the bottom of a very deep and stagnant fish tank. She's a figurehead, a title holder, a face to put on the money. She's got about as much impact on how Britain is run as the kid wearing the Dopey costume at Disneyland has on what Mike Eisner orders for lunch. And now that the sun has set on the British Empire, her kids have nothing to do until she dies except ski, play polo, screw like rabbits, and squander the royal subjects' money.

Dennis Miller

The sex lives of the royals have always made Larry Flynt's screening room look like an ashram. They are a drooling band of libidinous flesh-happy boff monkeys who have stopped pulling their sword from the stone and started plunging it into everything else on the planet. What's the point of being king if you can't plow the serfs and commoners once in a while, huh?

And if the royal bloodline is supposed to produce progeny that are physical specimens worthy of the throne, then how do you explain those Jethro Bodine cereal bowls Prince Charles calls ears? I haven't seen acoustic organs that big since the last time I went to an Argent concert. And you know he'll probably get mad when he hears all this stuff I'm saying, and I don't mean on TV or from someone else, I mean he can hear me right now.

I think that if any good has come from the field day that the media has had with the trials and tribulations of the royal family, it's that it exposes them for what they are—human. And rather unimpressive humans at that.

When it comes down to it, I'm a hundred times more impressed with the guy who invented Post-it notes than I am with the whole royal family combined. I mean, at least he created something.

In fact, I think the Post-it note guy should have been the one sucking on Fergie's toes.

You know, this bullshit would never play over here in the colonies. Unlike the Brits, we turn over our royalty every four to eight years. Stateside we have a term for people who want to be king: paranoid schizophrenics.

So why do our orthodontically challenged cousins fall for it? Well, when the British taxpayers foot the bill for the royal clubfoots, what they're really paying for is their fairy tale. They want to think their money is being spent on glass slippers and pumpkins that turn into carriages and all sorts of handsome prince paraphernalia. Proletariat life over there is so dreary that they just want that fantasy, that dream.

So when they find out their money's being spent on soccer players who do use their hands, rubbers, and long distance calls to discuss Zen and the art of tampon reincarnation, well, naturally their approval rating is gonna drop faster than a pair of tube socks on Kate Moss.

You know, as governments evolve to provide the greatest good for the greatest number of people, the royal family has become a vestigial organ. Indeed, the royal family is Britain's appendix. And I say that as long as it doesn't flare up, you might as well keep it. But right now the royals are throbbing and provoking a radiating distraction. So send the surgeon in and be done with it.

Face facts. Britain has no practical purpose anymore except providing America with fashions, rock stars, the wonderful Emma Thompson, and that little bald fucker who pimped for Benny Hill.

God save the queen. Because, quite frankly, the rest of us can't be bothered.

Of course, that's just my opinion, I could be wrong.

Dennis Miller

Abortion

Now, I don't want to get off on a rant here, because basically this topic is a mine field . . . abortion. I couldn't be any more on tiptoe if this rant were being produced by George Balanchine.

This is *the* big debate. And I'm talking bigger than who was the better Darren on *Bewitched*.

Abortion is our nation's Final Jeopardy. And I'll wager, Alex, that if America fights another civil war, it will be about this.

And I would remind you that this is all from my perspective. The male perspective. A one-step-removed perspective because I will obviously never have to decide on whether or not I should have an abortion. And, by the way, my belief is that if men were the ones getting pregnant, abortions would be easier to get than food poisoning in Moscow.

Having men decide the fate of a woman's reproductive system makes about as much sense as asking Quentin Crisp to coach the Raiders.

All right, enough qualifying. Let's get on with it. There's no doubt that passions run high on both sides, and this issue has created a divide in this country not seen since Carly Simon last yawned in public.

The prevailing opinions on a woman's freedom to choose are going further to the right than a Greg Norman tee shot. Prolife activists attempt to paint anyone prochoice as having no morals.

On the other side of the ledger, prochoicers are tagging prolifers as crazed and backward Bible thumpers bent on running the lives of the people who disagree with them.

The truth, as always is the case in human endeavors, lies somewhere in between. As much as the advance scouts on either side of this issue might not want to admit it, good people do get abortions and other good people are pained by their decision to get one.

Where do I stand? Well, I'm like most of you. I presume there are far too many abortions performed in this country. And I also believe that at the end of the day, as much as I might disapprove, none of them are really any of my business.

Look, there are always going to be arguments on this issue, the debate will rage until the end of time no matter what the whim of the papal infallibility or politics of the decade, but the simple truth is that such a passionate and personal issue dictates that the choice be left to the individual.

And, you know, that's really all we can do. Because we're just human beings stumbling around in the dark, trying to get to the bathroom and kickin' the shit out of our shins on the way there.

Now, there're some things that all right-minded human beings should agree on. We should all agree that abortion should be legal in the case of rape, incest, and when the mother's life is at risk. That's just common sense.

But excluding that obvious assumption, everything else in the abortion arena is in play. There are many quagmires complicating this issue.

Religion . . . now, it seems that religion is most often the backboard for every bank shot put up by someone making it their business to get into your business.

Roman Catholic doctrine forbids abortion. Fine, take that into consideration when you make *your* decision. Right-to-life proponents contend that abortion is immoral. Fine, take that into consideration when you make *your* decision.

Another pothole in the road to a sensible approach to abortion is when does life begin? At conception? When a heartbeat is detected? At the first drawn breath? You know, for me it wasn't until last Tuesday; until then I was still just a sperm with an accountant.

Okay, okay, so those are the variables and there are obviously millions more variables that make each individual case unique. But the more you think about it and the more it makes your head spin, and the more confused you get trying to figure out somebody else's life for them, it becomes increasingly apparent that it has to be the call of the individual who is pregnant.

Because the collective, one way or another, won't have to suffer the consequences of that most personal of all decisions.

My fellow Americans, it is time to suck it up, look deep into your immortal soul if you believe you have one, and do the right thing. Have the courage and strength to live your own life by your own standards and stop trying to call the shots for everyone else. We all live with glaring inconsistencies, and sometimes when you see something going on right in front of you that offends you to the very core of your being, sometimes the best thing you can do is to walk away, because you know that's exactly what you'd want them to do for you.

There is only one judge on this one, and it's God, and you don't get to meet him until you go backstage after the play is over.

And believe me, you do not want to get a thumbs-down from the guy who created thumbs, all right? In the interim, everybody's got to tend their own garden vis-à-vis abortion. And remember, when it comes to your own body, only you wear the robes and only you carry the gavel.

Of course, that's just my opinion, I could be wrong.

Bill Clinton, Second Term

Well, it's been about five and a half years since
we've kicked the big guy's tires and said "We'll take it,"
and now it's time we threw him up on the rack and gave
him the standard 26-point check to try and find out
where the hell all those funny noises are coming from.

Of course, I'm talking about the President of the
United States, the man in charge of looking like
someone's in charge. I'm talking about Billy Bob
Clinton. How can a guy so chunky be so damn smooth?

Now, I don't want to get off on a rant here, but if
somebody were to make a life-sized replica of Bill
Clinton entirely out of margarine, WD-40, and banana
peels, it would still be less slippery than the original.

Many people thought that Bill Clinton's first election to the presidency was a sign that character was no longer an issue in choosing the leader of this country. It had been established that he had dodged the draft, smoked pot, and his marital vows contained all the fidelity of a Kenner Close 'n Play. In other words, he's most people. Talk about being judged by a jury of your peers. We found him guilty and sentenced him to eight years in a federal institution.

It's easy to joke about Bill Clinton as an aw-shucks hillbilly; hell, I've been skipping to that well for half a decade now. And while that's not an entirely inaccurate portrayal, it's as representative of the total Clinton package as "Octopus's Garden" is of *Abbey Road*.

For while on the one groping hand he might appear to be a mouth-breathing hick, on the other, he is more adept at slinging bullshit than a street sweeper in Pamplona.

Bill Clinton treats the truth like your mom treats the good china. There's never an occasion special enough to actually use it, although you can take it out and look at it once in a while.

Now, putting aside my personal distaste for a moment, let me say that I do believe our President is a compassionate man. Unfortunately, his good intentions and moist-eyed empathy are derailed with Amtrak-like regularity by his almost pathological need to be liked by all factions and by his attempts to turn every situation to his political advantage. Thus, he can support campaign finance reform while selling White House policy to the highest bidder, decry China's human rights record while granting them favored-nation status, and feel our pain while slashing welfare and food stamps. This guy is a limping contradiction. He wants it both ways more often than Dennis Rodman.

And in spite of every paradox, Clinton's popularity continues to rise. The man can do no wrong. It's astounding. I mean, Christ, he makes Ronald Reagan look like Steve Buscemi.

Let's face it, we as Americans are inexplicably attracted and attached to this guy. Of course he's not innocent of all the scandals he's been tied to, he's far from perfect, and we just don't know if we should trust him. But we keep sticking with him, hoping he'll eventually change. You know, in a nutshell . . . we're all Hillary.

The truth about Bill Clinton is that he has an infallible internal leveling bubble that makes him the perfect politician. He has a wonderful way of making you feel as if you're the only person in the room, unless, of course, you're at an orgy with him. And maybe all that he's really guilty of is using that impressive power to craft himself into the President we want and need, someone who's a reflection of our own flawed self-image.

Poll after poll shows that even though Americans find Clinton's character reprehensible, they think he's doing a fine job, which translates to: "Yeah, he's an unbelievable sleazebag, but the economy's good." You know, we may not like what Clinton does, but he's a larger-than-life manifestation of the compromises and concessions we all have to make and the lies we all have to tell ourselves every day so that we can keep going. Cynical? You betcha. But, fuck it, my stocks are going through the roof.

Disgusting as I may find certain aspects of Bill Clinton's character, I have to confess admiration for his astonishing resilience. Our president extricates himself from the most difficult situations with an ability that is nothing short of James Bondian. No matter how bad it looks for him, he always winds up escaping in the lifeboat with a gorgeous babe, a perfectly chilled bottle of Perrier-Jouet, and a big side order of chili fries. Yee-haw!

Of course, that's just my opinion, I could be wrong.

America's Obsession with Beauty

Boy, this country is looks crazy, isn't it?

Now, I don't want to get off on a rant here, but Americans are under the delusion that the sublime physical perfection is the only way to get past the velvet ropes at Club Happy. We're exhausting ourselves in a narcissistic orgy of bingeing, purging, and free consultations, all in the hope that Father Time will cut us the same deal that Dick Clark has.

Now, at the Academy Awards, almost as important as who wins, hell, maybe even more important than who wins, is what are the women wearing. Women's gowns are analyzed, critiqued, and discussed as though this were the Potsdam Summit.

Models and movie stars are the aesthetic benchmarks against which we measure ourselves, regardless of how unattainable their beauty may be without access to personal trainers, extensive cosmetic surgery, and pharmaceutical speedballs. That's why people go to plastic surgeons asking for Juliette Lewis's lips or Mel Gibson's eyes. And your plastic surgeon can even give you Michael Jackson's nose . . . *literally.*

Ask any little girl what she wants to be when she grows up. Chances are she won't say president or astronaut or doctor. Chances are she'll say "Supermodel." What does it say about our culture when Einstein's original draft of the theory of relativity fetches less at auction than what a flat-line electroencephalograph Giacometti statue gets to stroll down a runway? And for God's sake, isn't it about time we passed an absolute edict forbidding these women from uttering the words "Modeling is hard work."

You know, women in our culture, however, find themselves deluged by mixed messages that leave them more rattled than a cocktail shaker in a Noël Coward play. Nowhere is this more evident than in women's magazines. I know that men have their *Esquires* and *GQs*, but, come on. A few pages of gay guys in clothes you would never wear, fifty features about sports and cars, and an article about how much chicks really dig love handles. Nobody gets hurt and the status quo is maintained.

Pick up a women's magazine and you're privy to the kind of brainwashing that would make the director of *The Manchurian Candidate* envious. A glance through one of these tony tomes and you're indoctrinated into a no-win mindfuck parallel universe populated by spindly, overpaid nineteen-year-olds in thousand-dollar frocks, hair and makeup tips so intricate they would confound Oppenheimer, and diets that make the rations at a Sudan refugee camp look like the Viennese table at Pavarotti's wedding. And the biggest irony is, in every single one of these magazines, there are at least five articles about how important it is to like yourself just the way you are.

Y'know, we're conditioned, weaned on, and addicted to "looking like" rather than actually "being" or "feeling." The fact that we prize beauty is the reason that we live in a perpetually disposable society. We worship something that is nothing but transitory. The standards for beauty have changed more over the ages than the names tattooed on Johnny Depp's arm.

One of the most recent beauty gotta-haves is big, full, pouting lips. And it's really easy. The doctor takes a syringe full of fat from your rear end and injects it into your lips. . . . Well, kiss my own ass, why didn't I think of that?

The fat injection takes care of the fullness, and the doctor's bill takes care of the pouting. Results vary. Some women leave looking like Steven Tyler after a bar fight.

A generation of movies and magazines has convinced many intelligent women to have their breasts enlarged. Now, many women in L.A. seem to take it to the nth-cup degree and they end up looking like something little Mexican kids should be whacking with sticks for candy and toys.

And if you don't want to get surgery, you can now buy the Wonderbra, which pushes your tits together like Japa-

Dennis Miller

nese subway riders at 7:45 A.M. And as with any money-making innovation, soon there are knockoffs. First there was the Wonderbra, then Victoria's Secret came out with The Miracle Bra, and there's even the Gossard Super-Uplift bra, which is not only a wonderful undergarment, but I believe also set a transatlantic crossing record in the mid thirties.

Oh, and by the way, Wal-Mart just came out with their own version, it's called the Hey, Lurleen, them ain't your titties bra.

And as far as body retooling goes, men are just as guilty as women. Some guys actually pay money to have somebody suck the fat out of their stomach and inject it into their penis. And you know what it cost? It cost $8432 and 25 cents. Worth every penny.

Men are also just as obsessed with what's missing from the top of their big heads. And I'm sorry to report to the follicly challenged that you're not fooling anybody with those mini-micro-mega grafts. If you leave work on Friday bald and come back on Monday looking like your sister's Skipper doll after a trip to Three Mile Island, we know what you did, squid attack-head.

Look, I have no problem with people who choose not to go gently into that saggy night. I don't think there's anything wrong with a little cosmetic surgery or primping and preening, as long as the external procedure isn't an attempt to make up for some internal flaw. Just don't rely on it to make you happier or expect it to make you a better person. To tell you the truth, lately I've been thinking about getting a little liposuction myself because uh, well . . . let's just say my belly button's not as close to my spine as it used to be. But, hey, come on, gimme a break, I have two kids and you know that can be hell on a man's body.

Of course, that's just my opinion, I could be wrong.

Parenthood

Ah, kids. You know usually I regale you with something that is nagging me about the modern world. But I would like to talk about something beautiful for a change. I'm talking about the joys of children.

Now, I don't want to get off on a rant here, but along with marrying my wife, having my two sons, Holden and Marlon, is the most important thing I have ever done or will ever do. Before you ask, yes, it's even more important than receiving my ACE awards, the award for cable excellence.

Now, nothing turns an adult inside out like having children. Our biological need to reproduce is stronger than the dining room chairs at Pavarotti's house.

You know, there comes a time in life where it just feels natural to procreate. For my wife and me that time came when I had mastered every level of Donkey Kong, there was a baseball strike, and they took *M.A.N.T.I.S.* off the air. What the hell else was I to do?

Then one day my wife told me, ah, she was pregnant. At that moment I went through more emotions than Jack Paar with low blood sugar. Believe it or not, I was speechless. But that didn't last. Primal guttural man pride took over. And I leapt to my feet, shouting, "I am a superhero! I am the Progenitor, Master of Fertility! Silly earthlings, your attempts to run from my seed are futile! You cannot hide from the life-giving molten baby juice of the Progenitor!" And then the maître d' asked me to sit back down because I was scaring the other diners. But bottom line— I was secure in the knowledge my dick worked.

Then after you have the baby, you suddenly find yourself so consumed with love that it all becomes quite simple: YOU WILL DO ANYTHING FOR YOUR CHILD. Your life becomes an endless round of sleep-deprivation, viewings of *The Little Mermaid,* and obsessive worrying about whether the baby-sitter worships Satan. Nothing is as precious to you as your child's physical and mental well-being. Since becoming a parent, I, who once dreamed of tooling around Monte Carlo in my Aston-Martin, breaking the hearts of wealthy contessas while insouciantly playing baccarat, have purposely lost more games of Candy Land to my kid than Brando threw prize fights in *On the Waterfront.*

Babies are wrinkled, they drool, they can't eat or go to the bathroom on their own, and they constantly need to take naps. When you think about it, they're like tiny little Bob Doles.

And by the way, shouldn't there be some kind of relationship between how much a baby eats and how much comes out the other end? For God's sake, it's like at the circus, where they've got the tiny VW bug but the clowns just keep coming out and out and out. . . . Eventually you learn how to hold your breath like a Hokkaido pearl diver.

Now, there are some minor frustrations attendant to children. Like children's music. All I can say is the wheels on the bus go round and round . . . and round and round and round. I don't know why that's so fascinating to kids. I mean, that's what wheels are supposed to do, go round and round. So why write a fucking song about it?

And what is it about the word "shit"? My son Holden heard me say it one day and he now repeats it nonstop. I hear the word shit more than a night manager at a Jack in the Box in Puerto Vallarta. Of course the problem with little children that modern science, NASA, or Bill Gates just can't seem to solve is that they grow up. One day you've got a little princess who thinks her daddy is a knight in shining armor, the next thing you know she's got a tattoo of Courtney Love on her back and she's in the driveway tongue-kissing a guy named Cyclops on a Harley while you're frantically trying to locate Mr. Peabody for a quick spin in the way-back machine.

Hey, there are no hard, fast rules about children, but here are some things you should know about raising kids that will make it easier for you.

Children leave food on all furniture and rugs. That's their job. It's an either-or proposition. You can't have kids and have nice things.

Don't try to be the hip parent. All my friends who had hip parents ended up getting into really hard drugs.

Here's why. When we enter our teens we want to rebel against our parents. But if your parents are rebellious themselves, then you have to work that much harder to get fucked up more than them. All right?

Show your spouse affection around the kids. Sometimes we become so harried, we forget to be affectionate around the children and they grow up assuming that all marriages are loveless. Think about it. Nobody in the audience tonight can even imagine their parents fucking. You know why? Because none of us can even imagine our parents looking at each other when they talked.

And be an adventurous parent. Don't be afraid that you're doing permanent damage. *You are* doing permanent damage. All humans are flawed goods. There's no getting around it. You are going to ruin your kid no matter what you do, so sit back and enjoy the ride, Mr. B.

In a nutshell, just be good and kind to your children because not only are they the future of the world, they are the ones who can eventually sign you into the home.

You know, yesterday evening I turned to my son at the dinner table and I said, "Eat your broccoli or no dessert." And then it hit me. I am irrevocably a parent. Once you utter those exact words to your kid, there's no turning back.

Dennis Miller

Eat your broccoli or no dessert is the official password that opens up an eighteen-year labyrinth strewn with nitroglycerine-encrusted Fabergé eggs that parents try to navigate in a pair of Elton John Pinball Wizard boots. And you know what, I would not trade it for the universe. It is the reason that I am here.

As long as I live—on this planet, I mean, not just on HBO—I will never forget my youngest son Marlon's first words.

One day I was sitting in the kitchen reading the newspaper and he toddled over to me, looked up, and said, "Yo, Perry White, how's about putting down that fish wrap and doin' a little turnover on the Huggie here. This little shit-Speedo's more full of crap than Rush Limbaugh." And all I could think was "Yup, that's my boy!"

Of course that's just my opinion, I could be wrong.

Modern
Psychology

Do you realize they have psychiatrists for dogs now? That in and of itself can screw up a dog. "Hey, pal, am I allowed up on the couch or am I not allowed up on the couch?"

Now, I don't wanna get off on a rant here, and I wouldn't, but I can't help myself, because, you see, I'm *addicted* to ranting and I am not responsible for my actions right now because I have what they call PCRS—pay cable rant syndrome. Somebody call Leslie Abramson and find me somebody to sue!

Let's face it, folks, as far as therapeutic introspection goes, we've become a nation of such insufferably unbridled me-monkeys, every hiccup of our psyche, every aberrant twinge of our consciousness no matter how insignificant, has become a springboard for the kind of fervent discussion and speculation that used to be reserved for Zapruder footage and the Sgt. Pepper album cover.

It seems to me that we are on some mission to discover every deep-rooted reason for being unhappy. We employ sophisticated therapies to plumb the depths of our very psyches. The first thing it seems people have difficulty grasping is the simple premise that life often just *is not fun*. Okay, I suppose the pursuit of happiness seems ofttimes almost as tragic and futile a gesture as the loading of the ice-making machine onto the *Titanic*.

Today we spend more time on our therapists' couch than on our own two feet. Psychotherapists are now the skycaps of our emotional baggage, except they're getting $150 tips and putting our bags on a flight that never seems to land. We have 12-stepped over the line, people.

I mean, back in ancient civilization there was no psychoanalysis. The only treatment they had then for depression was the plague. You knew why you were blue, because everybody on your fucking continent had just died.

You know, I would put more faith in psychotherapy if it weren't so susceptible to every goofy trend that rolls down the Mental Health Freeway. Let's look at some of the basic and not so basic options.

Now, some people are so eager to Scotchgard themselves from taking personal responsibility, they conveniently blame the shit in their lives on shit that supposedly happened to them in their past lives. Given the quality of American schooling, most people's knowledge of world history is so spotty that invariably, they can only claim in their past lives to have been either Cleopatra or Bob Dole.

Next, we have couples therapy. Now, the trick to picking a couples therapist is finding one who will side with you and not your wife. As any good shrink will tell you, there is no point in you going in for counseling if you're not going to go in there and give it all you've got to try and win, win, win.

In group therapy you get all the embittered losers together so they will have someone to talk to. Hey, isn't that called the back room at the post office?

The practice of aromatherapy makes the claim that smelling certain essential oils can help you overcome anxiety, depression, and stress. The theory that exposure to pleasant fragrances helps create a happy mood goes a long way toward explaining why the French are so cranky all the time.

Then, of course, there's pharmaceutical therapy. It has been established for some time that drugs can have a tremendous effect on a person's mood. Many people at different times in their lives have experimented with drug therapy, it's just that the "therapist" was then some guy named "Weiner" that lived down the hall and carried a four-finger Baggie in his tube sock.

Listen, I'm all for psychotherapy, I have more unresolved guilt than Gil Garcetti's office, and I'd venture a guess that over the years I've logged more frequent-fetish miles than most of you. After extensive therapy, I have concluded that I have the worst Oedipal complex in the history of psychoanalysis. I'm actually in love with Oedipus. Every summer I go to Greece looking to sodomize an old blind Greek guy.

In an age where science has triumphed over religion, psychotherapists have become our shamans, our exorcists, and our parent confessors. They are privy to our most intimate secrets, things we can't, or won't, tell lovers, families, or spouses. And in exchange for performing the distasteful task of rummaging through the rancid, cobwebbed, appallingly personal contents of our cranial Dumpsters and tilting quixotically at the windmills of our minds, they charge us prices that are steeper than the heels on The Artist Formerly Known As Prince's wedding pumps.

So, do you think you need therapy?

Well, if you're out on a date and you think everything is going well, and you're talking and talking and laughing and laughing and smiling and your date turns to you and for what seems like no reason she asks "You're not going to hurt me, are you?" . . .

Listen, maybe we're not supposed to know the dark secrets of self. Just accept the fact that the thought of being spanked with an empty Elmer's glue bottle turns you on. Accept it. Impulse is what keeps life interesting. Freudian peccadilloes are not necessarily bad. Think about it. Centuries ago some guy in Holland got off on the way wood felt on his feet. . . .

You know, the ocean of life is full of swells and not-so-swells and you have to ride them out. You don't need Prozac because somebody flamed you in the X-Files chat room, okay. You don't need Zoloft because Darcel from *Solid Gold* never answered your fan letter.

Your parents fucked you up. Get over it. Let it go. A parent's job is to prepare you for the rest of your life by fucking with your head.

So at the end of the day you know what the big answer is, the solution to the entire problem?! Well, what it is is . . . oh, I'm sorry, our time is up. We'll continue with this next week.

Of course, that's just my opinion, I could be wrong.

Dennis Miller

Elections

2/16/96

See the New Hampshire debate last night, huh, among the eight remaining Republicans? I think it's a bad sign that the most frequently used phrase in the debate was "I know you are, but what am I?"

It's another presidential election year, and as we careen toward our quadrennial first Tuesday after the first Monday in November goatfuck, we once again get to watch a sweaty gaggle of Republican nozzleheads engage in exactly the same kind of foul, shameless, vulgar sack race that the Democratic nozzleheads engaged in four years ago. All these politicians are interchangeable. That's why the American voter feels as frustrated as a choking victim at a Christian Scientist's award dinner.

Now, I don't want to get off on a rant here, but elections on every governmental level are now Pyrrhic wars of attrition. Potential candidates must run a gauntlet tighter than Phyllis Diller's forehead. You know any real leader won't even get in the game, leaving Americans with a choice between desiccated party apparatchiks, megalomaniacal bazillionaires, and totalitarian fanatics who think that Pol Pot deserves a posthumous MacArthur grant.

If you want to run, all you need is enough cash to get your platform seen by everybody and enough savvy to craft a brazenly hollow message that cuts like an itty-bitty book-light beacon through everybody else's brazenly hollow message.

And money is just the coal that feeds the Bessemer converter inferno that is mass media.

Television is a continuously expanding black hole of filthy lucre and misinformation. Most current candidates choose a negative advertising campaign. Negative advertising is mean-spirited, intellectually dishonest, and, most important, brutally effective. Just ask Barry Goldwater about the mushroom cloud that ate his career. He's installing cable in Scottsdale right now.

Y'know, negative campaigns work on television because there is no way to answer them. It's like ticktacktoe. The person that goes first always wins. And the public devours it like Hannibal Lecter on a refugee boat leaving Cuba.

Let's cut to the chase. In present-day America, clueless politicians compete for baseless votes cast by uninformed citizens for frighteningly irrational reasons.

Our moral standards are so low and the intellectual field so barren that if John Wayne Gacy rose from the dead tomorrow, he could put on his clown suit, hire Roger Ailes, and get enough name-recognition votes in New Hampshire to knock Dick Lugar out of the race. And then Dick Lugar could drop his alias, reenter the real world, and go back to his given name, Cock Beretta.

Why are Americans so disinterested in politics? Because we *can* be. Democracy is voluntary.

And our lack of interest hasn't happened overnight. It can be traced directly back to our ever-decreasing attention spans. We need anything politically important rationed out like Pez—small, sweet, and coming out of a funny plastic head.

You know, folks, the truth is, really great men never run for President. That's because the mere act of running for President makes you less than great.

Anybody who is willing to endure the indignity of putting his life as well as his family's privacy in the line of fire on the off chance that forty million Americans will see fit to elect him, well, that automatically makes him an asshole.

Only an asshole would want to sit through a five-hour state dinner for the President of Estonia.

Only an asshole would expect his wife to gaze blankly and Stepford-smile while he outlines some bogus plan to use private funding for Strom Thurmond's annual carbon-14 test.

And only a narcissistic asshole would think that he could bring this crazy quilt of 250 million self-centered assholes together. By being all things to all assholes.

As long as a candidate can't be pinned down, he'll win the office. He must feign competency without actually acting in any way where success or failure could be proven. It must look like he is constantly doing something while accomplishing nothing.

Like Vanna White in a power tie. This is the signature of a successful modern-day politician. This is how a politician stays in office.

And politicians today who do get elected to office always have their eye on reelection, turning them into fifty-year-old Eddie Haskells.

"Gee, that's a nice tax plan, Mr. Voter, gee, that's a lovely position on welfare, Mrs. Voter."

Well, you know something, I want the human being representing my country to be just that, a human being. Not a robot, not an android, not some animatron. He should be someone who's alternatingly bold and scared shitless, like we all are. I want someone who smoked pot, I want someone who got laid. I'm sick and tired of our Presidents being these half-formed body snatcher pods that turn up in Jeff Goldblum's mud bath.

Hey, if you look hard enough, you're gonna find a reason not to elect anyone.

Bob Dornan is so insane that he actually undersells Crazy Eddie.

Pat Buchanan. Okay, forget the fact that his chief aide keeps Hitler's missing testicle in his inside coat pocket. Buchanan is further to the right than a bicyclist on the autobahn. Pat Buchanan is a registered trademark of the National Rifle Association and cannot be used without their express written consent.

Morry Taylor. Hmmm, should I vote for Morry Taylor or should I vote for Mel Cooley. No, no, maybe I'll vote for Larry Tate and his running mate, Dr. Bellows.

Lamar Alexander's about a month and a half away from playing Norm to Jimmy Carter's Bob Vila. At least Alexander is insightful enough to realize that the current American electorate are such chronic droolers that they would actually vote for a fucking shirt.

Bob Dole. I don't know if I want a President who is congratulated on his birthday by Willard Scott.

And finally, how can I vote for Dick Lugar when he doesn't even have the courage to use his real name, Schlong Uzi.

Of course, that's just my opinion, I could be wrong.

Sportsmanship

3/15/96

What the hell happened to our formerly pastoral pastimes? Sports in this country. Owners are rapacious and disloyal, players are spoiled, ill-mannered lowlifes, coaches are abusive psychopaths, hot dogs are $6.50. . . .

Now, I don't want to get off on a rant here, but the level of sportsmanship in America is dropping faster than the balance in Steve Forbes's daughters' trust funds. If I see one more athlete make a routine play and do a wild banshee itchy dance, I'm going to slap the man senseless with my remote, strap him in the Tony Burgess chair, toothpick his eyes open, and make him watch a little bit of the old Nike ultracommercialism till he pukes.

Today's athletes are so wrapped up in the entertainment aspect of sports, they can't complete the most basic of tasks without performing some kind of field, ego-driven, self-congratulatory ritual that makes ESPN's *Plays of the Day* look like that newsreel footage of Mussolini being oh-so-pleased with himself. Football players dance after sacks, they dance after touchdowns, they dance after they put their goddamn cup on. I bet just out of habit even O.J. did an end-zone dance and spiked the knife into the ground when he was finished.

I mean, if I have to see Neon Deion Prime Time Do-Rag Video Game Rap Album Krugerrand-Necklace Wearing Pizza Hut Two Sport Sanders high-stepping into the end zone like some kind of Bob Fosse–trained Nazi one more time, I think I'm gonna do the icky shuffle right off a fuckin' cliff.

Bad sportsmanship has now become just another attitude. I mean, somewhere along the way winning became not enough. All of a sudden not only did you have to win, you had to make your opponent look bad in the process. You know the attitude, you stand like a statue at home plate watching the ball sail out of the park, you hover over the quarterback you just sacked and point your finger in his face, or you drag an unsuspecting child out of the stands onto the court and threaten him with a bucket of water that you know is really filled with confetti. Damn you, you evil Globies. Damn you to hell.

And today's fans aren't much better either. Their rudeness makes it impossible to go to the stadium and enjoy the game. For example, why is it at every football game, even in Buffalo, where it's twenty below in the sun, there's always that guy in the stands with no shirt on?

And you know, the guy that takes his shirt off at the football game is always the guy that *really really shouldn't*, okay. Not only should this guy be wearing a shirt, he should be wearing a bra. *He* is why shirts were invented in the first place. He's a huge fat guy with big tits, folks, and he's standing on his chair with a giant beer in one hand and a pile of nachos in the other, no plate, just nachos in his hand, and he's screaming Thurman Thomas's name for sixty straight minutes. And you know what? I don't even think he knows Thurman Thomas. And the announcers say, "There's a real Bills fan, he's painted his body Buffalo Blue." Hey, that's not paint, the guy's dying of exposure. How can the fans enjoy the game when a huge fat guy with big tits is turning blue and dying right in front of them? They can't! At least, not like they could if a huge fat guy with big tits turning blue and dying right in front of them wasn't there.

An ends-justifies-the-means mentality seems to have infected all aspects of American life. We're fixated on success at any price, even if it means winning uglier than Charles Laughton after a chemical peel. Sportsmanship, decency, honesty, and fair play are all paid about as much attention as Moneypenny at a Bond girls' reunion.

If we look at society as a huge dysfunctional family, then the relationship we have with our professional athletes resembles one between a codependent spouse and the abuser. In our minds, despite all we've accomplished as adults, we're still the pathetic little twerps who got picked last for all the dodge-ball games, and we're still so desperate to be accepted by the jocks that we're willing to let them sit on us during lunch and fart right in our faces. We take their abuse because that way, we're sure that they know we love them.

Dennis Miller

And we continue to buy the double-decker tacos and antiperspirant they hawk, and allow ourselves to be gouged ever deeper on ticket prices, and condone the kind of off-the-field misconduct that would get you 86'd from Caligula's mailing list.

What does it say about us when we confer hero status on a guy just because he can play a game. Why wasn't O.J. properly disciplined the first time he ever slapped his wife around? What about the second time or the third? The fortieth or the fiftieth? It's time to wake up and smell the overpriced peanuts, the fossilized popcorn, and the syrup-needs-adjusting lukewarm soda and realize that the same standards for behavior apply to everyone, and that a wife-beating thug is a wife-beating thug whether he lives in a mobile home full of bowling trophies or a mansion full of Heisman Trophies.

We've given these monsters life, and we cut them more slack than the jaws of the studio audience at a taping of *Hee-Haw,* and you know something? It has got to stop. If these guys are to be treated like heroes and paid like heroes, well, then, goddammit, they should act like heroes. Wealth and adulation carry a price.

So, let me propose some very simple rules, rules we're all *supposed* to adhere to but somehow, just like in high school when the guys on the football team got to skip assembly on the day of the big game, pro athletes seem to be oftentimes immune to:

When you're on the clock, give it all you've got, be a magnanimous winner and a gracious loser. When you're off the clock, don't carry weapons, don't get into fistfights with fans, don't expose yourself in public, get your blowjobs from people who are of legal age, don't drive recklessly, stay away from the Bolivian marching powder, don't pull a gun on civilians, don't gamble illegally, and pay your fucking taxes.

All right, that takes care of the Dallas Cowboys.

Of course, that's just my opinion, I could be wrong.

The Prison System

Now, I don't want to get off on a rant here, but our prison system is as out of control as Billy Idol on Ecstasy at the Hawaiian Tropic finals. The day a convicted child murderer can give the family of the victim the finger is the day our system of punishment is as worthless as the man who gave it.

Premium cable, weight rooms, basketball courts, and conjugal visits, amazingly enough, have not thrown a paralyzing fear of returning to prison into the habitual offender. No. Criminals don't fear prison for the simple fact that life there is often the same if not, for some of them, better than the life outside.

Prison is getting way too costly. It has been estimated that keeping a guy behind bars can cost upward of $20,000 a year. You know, it would be a lot cheaper just to put him in a Motel 6.

Because of the current Get Tough on Crime campaign, policies like Three Strikes and You're Out, and the fact that many of the Clintons' friends have recently been getting caught, overcrowding has become epidemic in our prisons, with two men often sharing an eight-by-ten-foot cell. Well, you know what? People in New York City pay handsomely to live in similar conditions, except in Manhattan, when you don't even get the courtesy of a pack of cigarettes for your trouble, all right?

Our system actually lets inmates sue if they don't like the guards or the food or the work or the reception on the giant screen TV. Why are they able to sue? They *broke* the law, they shouldn't get to *use* it anymore.

The purpose of a prison is to protect the community from bad people. And let's get that cleared up too. These *are* bad people. There comes a time in your life when you just don't have time for excuses and you have to cut through all the bullshit and say there is good and there is evil and some people choose to be good and some people choose to be evil. Many people who are sent to prison, even though they may have been molested, beaten, and deprived of the recommended daily dose of folic acid when they were kids still made a choice to be evil. And it's very easy under the guise of compassion to say that these prisoners should be given perks.

But where, may I ask, is the compassion for the victim? My compassion begins and ends with the person wearing the toe tag. And trust me, you out there who have yet to lose your Billy Jack cherry, your sense of compassion is going to change dramatically once you're staring down the business end of a sawed-off shotgun while some foul-smelling extra-Y-chromosomed feral Gary Killmore wanna-be is demanding a week's salary out of your cash register. Suddenly all bets are off. And you're changing your tune faster than Elvis Costello on *Saturday Night Live*. You'll want that guy convicted, and when he gets to prison you'll want him passed around like a joint at the Dennis Hopper estate.

You know, there's a big brouhaha over bringing back chain gangs. The ACLU says chain gangs violate the human rights of prisoners. Oh, yeah?

Where was the ACLU when the prisoner was violating the human rights of the guy whose head he cut off with an ax? You've got upward of a thousand men in a confined space with energy to burn. . . . I say you put 'em to work. Our infrastructure's crumbling, our beaches are filthy, public buildings are in disrepair, my koi pond needs a good skimming. . . . We are ignoring a valuable source of free labor. Hell, think of how many Kathie Lee Gifford jogging suits the population of Sing Sing could sew in one day.

You know, the problem with liberal prison-reform advocates is they confuse "tough" with "inhumane." Denying prisoners privileges like cable TV and *Penthouse* magazine and feeding them crappy food isn't inhumane.

For God's sake, those are the kind of conditions I faced every week when I was a comic on the road. Look, prison is not supposed to be fun. It's not supposed to be pleasant. *It is prison!*

All right, don't put minor drug offenders in prison, I'll grant you that. Putting someone in prison for possession of drugs is like putting Tommy in a sensory dep-tank. It doesn't make sense. There are more drugs in prison than there are at a potluck at William Burroughs's house. And marijuana offenders should definitely not be put in with the most violent criminals. Have a separate pothead wing where they can gather and watch cartoons all day or play hacky-sack in the yard.

And I don't believe in just warehousing people.

Don't get me wrong, it would be great if we could, but they aren't square enough to stack well. Perhaps we should look into a system like the dry cleaners have. We just put 'em on hangers in alphabetical order, after a while we go in with a claim ticket, the line whizzes around till we get to the right one, we check carefully to see if they got the stain out, and if not, back into the fucking dryer.

I believe in affording options, just don't be stupid about it. There should be a pathway out for people who want to follow it, but it should be straight and narrow and every time you divert from it, even minimally, you get a swift kick in the ass, not another cookie.

You think prisoners should have privileges? Okay, but let's compromise. They want cable television? Fine, give 'em a twenty-four-hour feed of the security cam at the convenience store they knocked off.

Conjugal visits? Sure. Doesn't Leona Helmsley still have some community service to work off? Movies? Well, put your best black and white striped Wonderbra on, Richard Speck, because we just got the director's cut of *Nell*. You want a weight room? You got a weight room. It's spelled w-a-i-t. It's your cell, assface. Now get in it and wait.

Of course, that's just my opinion, I could be wrong.

The Death
of Common
Sense

You know, lately I find myself recurringly gripped by an overwhelming desire to smack our entire country upside its collective head.

Now, I don't want to get off on a rant here, but common sense in this country isn't just dead, it's been cremated and Woody Harrelson is smoking his ashes in his lucky skull bong. There is so little common sense today that Thomas Paine is spinning over in his grave so rapidly that they are thinking of hooking him up to a turbine to light up the Vegas strip.

You can't get to your office in the morning without colliding with some idiot who is trying to spawn upstream onto the elevator while everyone else is trying to get off.

You can't get in your car and not run into another idiot who pulls into the gas station with his fuel tank on the wrong side and then has to get instructions from a NASA team at Houston Control to figure out how to maneuver his car so that the tank is on the correct side. And you can't open a paper without reading about a mondo idiot who gets hurt or killed at a railroad crossing because they had to try and beat the train to get home in time to watch Charlene Tilton's salute to porcelain clowns on QVC.

Now, what the fuck has happened to us? A chalk outline is slowly being drawn around common sense and most Americans can't even identify the victim. We've gone from a nation of practical-minded, can-do Johnny-Get-Your-Guns and Rosie the Riveters to a bunch of sniveling crybabies who can't take it on the chin without running whining to our lawyers.

Christ, we're so bogged down in procedure, we make Radar O'Reilly look like Henry David Thoreau. You couple that with a Blanche DuBois-like denial of personal responsibility for the crap in our lives, and it's no wonder we're in a malaise that makes a bout of Epstein-Barr seem like a Laker Girl doing the Watusi after four triple lattes with a Dexatrim chaser.

You know, there's 800,000 lawyers in our country, and many of their livelihoods depend on the fact that we have *got* no common sense. My theory is that intelligence, like every other resource on this planet, has a finite amount. And as the population increases, the intelligence resource is being stretched thinner than the elastic in Marge Schott's G-string.

Ranting Again

For instance, some old lady burns herself on a cup of coffee at McDonald's and sues for three million dollars because it's not her fault. And she wins. She wins! We have trouble convicting people who actually confess to murder, but this woman is able to take three mil off of McDonald's? If the judge had any common sense, the trial should have gone like "Will the plaintiff please rise? Yeah, it is your fault. You're stupid. Coffee is supposed to be hot. Why didn't you blow on it before you chugged it down like a pledge having his first beer? Get out of my courtroom, you stupid, stupid woman and take your pin-striped parasite lawyer with you. Next case."

Common sense has been defined as the quality of judgment necessary to know the simplest of truths. Well, nowadays simple truths are sighted about as often as Mary Hart on *Crossfire*.

In the last twenty years we seem to have completely lost the ability to obey the natural laws around us. We no longer recognize things that are shockingly wrong anymore. We can't tell up from down, right from left, absolutely one hundred percent not guilty from double-murdering scumbag guilty. And we are getting stupider. Are we stupid or were we always this stupid?

I watch these TV evangelists on late-night cable channel 66 and see the stadium full of people giving hard-earned money away to some chrome-head, sweat-covered barking con man dangling eternal salvation in front of these poor bastards like a leash in front of a chihuahua with one kidney.

Well, I'm just shocked at our lack of our common sense. Clearly, this crook couldn't be more full of *shit* if he were a Porta Potti at the Lollapalooza festival.

Now, to many people the government is the main foundry of not-know-how, turning the raw ore sent to it by votes and tax dollars into cold-rolled sheets of incompetence, which are then used in every aspect of our societal infrastructure. Reports on reports of subcommittees of commissions create a sea of paper that could float Rush Limbaugh's butter dish. All in all, practicality has about as much chance of being served by the federal government as a loud Texan does by a French waiter.

Folks, we don't need more government, we don't need more colleges; we need more schools that teach common sense. We don't need any more Einsteins who can tell you the principle of microwave cooking but can't figure out how to plug one in. I've always said, "Give someone a fish and they'll eat for a day, teach someone not to run a bass lure through their testicle and they will be able to fish for the rest of their life."

Where does common sense come from? It's slapped into the back of your head by your mother when you try and touch the hot stove. It's the Oldsmobile crest branded onto your forehead for all of eternity because you didn't want the seat belt to wrinkle your new shirt. Common sense is what gores you in the ass in Pamplona when you dress up like Topo Gigio and run in front of

the bulls down a street that's narrower than Newt Gingrich's mind.

And most important, common sense is admitting
when you don't have a big closer. I don't have a big
closer.

Of course, that's just my opinion, I could be wrong.

L'Affaire O.J.

5/10/96

Now, I don't want to get off on a rant here, but it's about time to put the Bronco in reverse and take a long, slow look back at the Trial of the Century.

Since October 3, 1995, the verdict in the O. J. Simpson trial has reverberated in America's consciousness like the last chord of "A Day in the Life" played on a perpetual tape loop inside a squash court. No amount of psychic sorbet seems to be able to cleanse our collective palate of the nasty taste left by l'Affaire Simpson. It lingers as stubbornly and unpleasantly as a drunken party guest passed out on the couch with an open bottle of Hai Karate in his pocket, and the questions that it's raised nag at us like Norman Bates's mom on a rainy Sunday.

You know, the Simpson jury didn't really "hand down" their decision, it's more like they pulled its pin and lobbed it at us. When the verdict was read, people did more double takes than Professor Irwin Corey at a Hawaiian Tropic competition.

And what have we learned from the trial now that we've chewed it over like Bob Dole gumming a wad of month-old saltwater taffy. Well? That the only way you'll ever get a trial by a jury of your peers in this country is if you happen to be ill informed and predisposed. I think some of these people made their minds up before the murder even happened. We also learned that if you're a black lawyer and you take a case where you are prosecuting a black man for a crime that you know in your heart he committed, it automatically makes you a sellout to your race. And we learned that if you're a convicted wife beater, it's okay to disgrace your dead spouse's memory by giving a sworn deposition where you say "She hit me first."

We also learned that empirical evidence doesn't seem to matter anymore. The sea of blood on the killer's hands and Bronco was so deep that it had its own undertow. The evidence was more overwhelming than a New York City taxi in August with all the windows shut. And how did Team O.J. combat that K-2–sized mound of proof? Well, their defense strategy involved more smoke and mirrors than a tire fire in a brothel.

Well, you know something, they didn't convince me. Because even if you Martinize away all the blood, you are still left with a womanizing, wife-beating, egotistical, drug-using, possessive bully. And just for that I think he should be locked away tighter than Gordon Elliott's cummerbund at the Daytime Emmy Awards.

Dennis Miller

You know, I blame a lot of what happened at the trial on Lance Ito. I mean, a judge is supposed to control a trial, but Ito had about as much command of the room as Kathie Lee Gifford singing "You Light Up My Life" at the Apollo Theater.

Oh, well, Ito's gone. There's a new ringmaster now that the circus has died down but not completely pulled out of the station. O. J. Simpson is currently embroiled in a wrongful-death civil suit that could eat up whatever money he's got left from the last trial and his jackals-for-the-defense didn't make off with. The videotape he was hawking to help pay his legal fees netted about as much as the Philly cheese-steak concession at a k. d. lang concert. His lame attempts at reviving his flagging career and his destroyed credibility are as transparent as a Vargas girl's nightgown. So what's an O.J. to do?

Hey, that book he wrote where he answered people's questions did pretty well. Maybe he could write an advice column called "Dear Stabby."

You know, at this point the fact is that it just doesn't seem to matter anymore to anyone that O.J. did it. It's no big deal, it's become just another punch line. He plotted it and planned it, worked out all the timing, his escape route, his alibi, and the only unscheduled stumbling blocks he had to improvise around were Kato wanting to go talk to the big clown and Ron Goldman wanting to not die. Like he once did with linebackers that stood between him and the end zone, O.J. got by them. In the words of that NFL films announcer: "On that warm June day a fierce warrior had a mission. That warrior was Orenthal James Simpson, a man possessed, a man who was not to be denied."

Ranting Again

He pulled a fancy stutter-step on Kato, then squared his shoulders and ran right over Ron Goldman. Penalty flags were thrown, but upon further review the referees in the black and white striped shirts actually turned out to be referees in black shirts and referees in white shirts.

I freely admit to feeling cheated that O. J. Simpson didn't get life for his crimes. That he probably will never be brought to his arthritic knees. I assuage my anger by reassuring myself that he will never again elicit the respect and admiration of reasonable people. That he'll always be whispered about like some latter-day Hester Prynne wearing an "M" instead of an "A." And that he will always be surrounded by black-slappers, sycophants, ass-kissing golfing buddies, and coke-whores who are looking to thrill-fuck a murderer.

Hey, you know what, folks, I think he did get life. . . . Yeah, he did . . . you're our bitch now, O.J.

Of course, that's just my opinion, I could be wrong.

The Pursuit
of Happiness

For crying out loud, we live in a country where "the pursuit of happiness" is written into the Declaration of Independence. We live in the land of Happy Meals. Happy Meals. You know, there are people living, barely, on this planet for whom a Happy Meal is when they find an extra dung beetle in their bowl of roots and twigs. I mean, c'mon, in a lot of those countries, fast food is a gazelle. So why, in this land if freedom and plenty, are we loaded to the gills with Zoloft? Why do more people miss work yearly due to depression than to any other physical malady? Why are we such alcoholic, sex-and-drug-addicted, bingeing-and-purging, compulsively gambling, ulcer-ridden basket cases?

Now, I don't want to get off on a rant here, but most Americans are sadder than Bob Vila's neighbor trying to sleep in.

I believe that as we grow up, we are actually taught to be unhappy. We are shown what we don't have, we learn that society places value on accumulating material possessions, and we find out that success means winning an award. Happiness and satisfaction go hand in hand and we can never be satisfied because goals have been set for us that are higher than the entire front row at Reggae Sunsplash '98.

And even if you've made your peace with the material world, even if your baseball team is half a game out of first place and your family is healthy, even if you've learned to accept your lot in life and tend to your little garden, how can anybody with a shred of compassion in their soul sit through five minutes' worth of network nightly news without feeling like Sylvia Plath during a screening of *Shoah* while listening to Neil Young's "After the Gold Rush"?

It's a brutal world. More than ever, tragedy, violence, mayhem, and injustice seem to be the order of the day. It's almost impossible to enjoy with a clear conscience whatever little piece of tranquillity you've carved out for yourself while abject misery and suffering is all over the world like phony on Kathie Lee Gifford.

You know, we have the unrealistic expectation that unless every nanosecond of our life is spent in multiorgasmic joy, we're being ripped off worse than the Von Trapp family in a New York City taxi from JFK into Manhattan.

The quest for happiness is a metaphysical game of three-card monte and we are both sucker and shill. We know we'll never find the red card, but a little voice inside us makes us keep throwing down twenties. Listen up, guys and gals, you may never be any happier than you are right now. You may be richer or better-sexed or more powerful, but *you may never be any happier.*

Our entire existence is spent yearning for what we don't have, and we're convinced that whatever it is we're missing is the one thing keeping us from perfect bliss, transcendence, nirvana, satori . . . whatever term your particular ideological affiliation uses for the state in which life truly resembles a lite beer commercial.

What makes people happy anyway? I've come to the conclusion that most people are only really happy not when something good happens to them, but when something *bad* doesn't happen to them. Remember how good you felt when your neighbor's house got struck by lightning because he got the new satellite dish?

We could go round and round on this all night, but that would fly in the face of what I've been trying to say all along. Happiness doesn't always require resolution.

But, rather, an in-the-moment, carefree acceptance of the fact that the worst day of being alive is much better than the best day being dead. And personally, I've never been happier than this precise moment because I just found out that an extensive two-week investigation by the federal government revealed no violations of child labor laws in the production of my new line of Dennis Miller active wear. You are gonna *love* my new sports bra.

Ranting Again   153

Hey, happiness is not settling for less, but just not being miserable with what is. I have always lived by the creed "It's not the approval or accolades or possessions that make you smile, but simply making the left turn even though you were the third car in the intersection."

I myself have learned to love the simple things.

Nothing makes me happier than coming upstairs and finding my wife sound asleep in bed with our two children. Covering them with Grandma's quilt, going downstairs to make sure all the doors are locked, stepping out onto my wood deck to a clear summer night with every star blazing brilliantly through a balmy breeze while I contemplatively run through my head a list of anyone who was ever a cast member of *Saturday Night Live* and try to figure out how their career is going compared to mine.

Of course, that's just my opinion, I could be wrong.

Dennis Miller

Spouses

You know, I read somewhere that Paul McCartney and his wife have never been apart for a single night since they've been married. That's kind of sweet, isn't it? Evidently, that's their approach to marriage—close proximity. But everybody has their own separate tack on how to stay with their spouse for the rest of their life.

Now, I don't want to get off on a rant here, but a great marriage is like a duck. On the surface it looks cool and effortless, but underneath, well, you know, everybody's paddling like hell.

So, why do you do it? Well, there comes a point in everyone's life when they sense the randomness, the utter chaos of the world, and begin to search for an anchor, someone whose presence will serve as a haven of comforting familiarity and, hopefully, regular sex in the tornado-beset trailer park that is our daily existence.

Unfortunately, in a time when even the most steady of us has the attention span of the guy from *Shine* hooked up to a Jolt Cola IV, preventing spousal familiarity from deteriorating into a rut that makes something look like something else . . . sorry the simile well is dry.

I want to qualify this by stating to all the menfolk out there that if you have a spouse as wonderful as the one I have, you should thank your lucky stars. Because between reasonably priced landscaping services, Jiffy-Lube, and sperm banks, men are . . . you know, men are pretty much optional nowadays. There are times when men feel only vaguely tolerated in a relationship, and there may be stretches when it seems like the only time you're not in hot water with your wife is when you take a shower after her.

The problem is that we go into marriage knowing about as much as our mates as Mia Farrow did in *Rosemary's Baby*. Or, for that matter, as much as Mia Farrow did in her actual life.

You know, some people would say that spouses can be separated into two stereotypically different groups. There are the remote-controlling, chore-ducking, boat-buying, beer-bellied, non-conversing, insensitive natural-gas factories called husbands. And then you have the mall-blazing, in-law-inviting, will-you-put-the-goddamn-toilet-seat-down, you-really-don't-remember-what-today-is-do-you, we-never-go-anywhere shoe junkies called wives.

Now, I obviously can't speak for women—I can periodically dress like them, and I will continue to do so, but here are some things that women should know about men that would make being married to them easier:

1. All husbands are losing their hair. Now, there is nothing a wife can do to make her husband feel better about that. So here's how you nip it in the bud, ladies. The first time your husband comes out of the shower pulling his hair back, asking if you think he's going bald, this is what you say: "You know darling, I'm looking at your dick right now, and to be honest, hair loss is the least of your problems."

2. All right, ladies, you know your friend from high school, Howard, who you always use as an example because he actually cleared the table and then put the dishes in the dishwater without even being asked? Howard is gay. Believe me. I met him one night when I was dressed as a woman.

3. Despite what you've been told, men love to cuddle after sex. But why does your head have to block the TV?

4. Don't sit down and watch Australian Rules football with us. You don't want to try to understand Australian Rules football. Nobody understands it. We don't understand it. All right? That's the whole point. When we are watching Australian Rules

football, it means we just went into our invisible he-man clubhouse. And you know that the only reason you sit down next to us and pretend you want to watch is that you want to come into our he-man clubhouse and ruin it with your girl cooties. So stay out. All right!

5. Husbands need to be asked to do something three times. The first time we don't even hear you, and the second time we don't think you mean it.

6. Gals, gals, you know that primordial sense of nurturing you get from raising children? Huh? That's the same way we feel about our baseball caps. Okay?

7. Finally, ladies, will you stop, please, stop trying to talk us into a threesome with your best friend. We're just not interested. Okay?! That's not what we're about.

You know the most important thing in a marriage? Huh? You want to know what it is? You must respect your spouse for who he or she is. Don't try to change them. In marriage, what you see is what you get. Sure, maybe one day your husband will love Jane Campion movies and be able to last more than seven minutes inside Bed, Bath, and Beyond without taking a salesclerk hostage with a fucking loufah. And maybe your wife won't wince when you tell the same three stories at a dinner party for the forty-seventh time, and maybe she will make left turns according to your specifications, but don't hold your breath, all right. It's learning to endure your spouse's little flaws, i.e., their maddeningly stubborn refusal to be exactly like you, that builds character.

Dennis Miller

Your spouse is someone that you can feel comfortable doing absolutely nothing with. Someone whose expectations are always softened by understanding. A completely different person through whose eyes, over time, you see yourself more clearly.

Of course, that's just my opinion, I could be wrong.

Lying

Now, I don't want to get off on a rant here . . . actually, that's a lie, I do want to get off on a rant here.

I'm talking about something that everybody does, nobody admits, and when they get caught doing it, they always have a good excuse. No, I'm not talking about laughing hysterically during *America's Funniest Home Videos,* I'm talking about lying.

Now, despite the bad rap lies get, can you imagine a world without them? I mean, it would be bedlam. The end of family get-togethers as we know them. First dates never even making it to the restaurant. Toupee makers all out of business. Chaos.

And the weird thing is, we even lie to other animals. I mean, come on, who here hasn't faked out a dog by only pretending to throw the tennis ball? You think that's a cute trick, a little game? Uh, it's a big fat lie, and don't think your dog doesn't know it. Oh, sure, he might fall for it the first five or six hundred times, but then he'll catch on.

I think most reasonable people wouldn't deny that some lies are harmless little isolated episodes of convenient untruth. Gentle inaccuracies like: "Hey, a lime-green paisley tie, great!" Or "This mutton sorbet is delicious"; and "Hey, that was really fun. Sure, I'll call."

But lying is so commonplace, we've become hardened to it, and we even expect it. For God's sake, we've just reelected a president who we all know is a complete, bald-faced, unadulterated . . . all right, strike unadulterated . . . unmitigated bullshit artist. And sadly, what Bill Clinton has done so far in his career is no different from what any politician throughout history has done. You show me an honest politician, and faster than you can say "Dukakian landslide defeat" I'll show you a guy who'll be teaching poli sci at a community college in Light-my-fart, Arkansas.

Our collective mind-set is so mistrustful, we make Laurence Harvey in *The Manchurian Candidate* look like Papa Smurf. With the proliferation of *X-Files* Web sites and conspiracy theories on everything ranging from Vince Foster's suicide to Susan Lucci's never winning an Emmy, paranoia has become a national cottage industry.

But loath as we are to admit it, you know, we need lies. Lying is the WD-40 on the gears of our lives. Without the regular dissemination of fibs, whoppers, and just plain bullshit, our lives would derail like an Amtrak train under ideal conditions.

Lying is the horns, claws, and teeth that we weren't born with. Once we found out we could hunt animals by trickery, the tool of deception became our sharpest stick and we soon learned to turn it on each other. To this day the ability to lie remains the most well-oiled wrench in our box.

Okay, perhaps it's a bit harsh to call all of us liars. Whatever you prefer. Fact reconstructionist . . . Truth manager . . . Reality stylist . . . Whatever you want.

Unfortunately, the vast majority of our public figures seems incapable of telling the difference between white lies, gray lies, and lies so black, they could suck the light from Las Vegas and still have enough black left over to provide a lifetime supply of turtlenecks to the Yale English department.

And then there's my business. Show business. You look for honesty in show business, you might as well be looking for Parliament Funkadelic albums at Mark Fuhrman's house. L.A. is to dishonesty what Wisconsin is to cheese. In Hollywood, lying to someone is simply considered to be good manners. It's the town where "Let's do lunch" actually means "You're dead to me, assface."

The truth is that the truth has become more malleable than Stretch Armstrong in a Navajo sweat lodge.

The truth used to be the Holy Grail. The truth used to be the brass ring, the mint-condition Babe Ruth rookie baseball card with the original stick of gum still intact. But, my friends, you may officially consider the gum to be chewed and stuck under the theater seat.

Remember, the bottom line is this, lying merely for personal gain or benefit is morally and ethically wrong. And I feel I can say that with all integrity and conviction to you, the smartest book purchasers that I have ever written for in my entire life, I love you all.

Of course, that's just my opinion, I could be wrong.

Art

You know, most older philanthropists end up giving their money to the arts. Or at least they used to, when art was still art. Now, I'm not an art aficionado by any means. Until recently I thought Chagall was once married to Kelly LeBrock.

But I'd like to think that I have an eye for aesthetics, the symbols that stir and inspire—meaning one thing to you and something else entirely to another. . . . But let's cut to the chase—SHIT IS SHIT, no matter how you frame it.

Now, I don't want to get off on a rant here, but what is art? Art is a combination of feelings and the talent to express those feelings through painting or sculpture or architecture or whatever medium. Who knows? I mean, I may have had some of the same feelings as Michelangelo, the difference being he expressed his with the statue of David and I express mine by talking to M&Ms.

You know, art used to be simple. You saw something pretty, or scary, or holy, and you recreated it using whatever you had lying around. You weren't a "pre-modern minimalist expressionist primitivist," you were a Neanderthal in a cave, drawing a fucking horsey. And when you were done, all the other cave dwellers didn't stand around drinking fermented berry juice and eating mastodon milk cheese and discussing the rhythm and nuance of your composition and the subtle texturing of the dung you used.

Until photography came along in the mid-1800s, artists were essentially little Brownie cameras hanging from a strap around the neck of the privileged elite who wanted their estate and family to be preserved for posterity.

Walk through any museum and what you pretty much see is paintings of rich bastards and their stuff. But once the camera came into existence, it freed artists up to give their impressions rather than record precisely what they saw. And that's when the LeRoy Neiman hit the fan.

Cut to the present-day art world: an incestuous society of toadies, charlatans, and wanna-Kostabis who are more interested in perpetuating the myth of their own talents than actually producing anything that's even remotely aesthetically pleasing.

The purest distillation of this snobbery is performance art. Refuge of the untalented, repository of more pretentiousness than the diary of a fifteen-year-old girl on her first trip to Paris.

For those of you who are fortunate enough never to have come in contact with performance art, imagine every awful poet, annoying mime, gratingly unfunny comedian, unappetizing drag queen, and embarrassingly inept singer all merged into one narcissistic artiste with a bad haircut and absolutely no sense of shame, braying his or her incomprehensible message into the TriBeCa night. Art? Well, you didn't think of doing it, did you?

And isn't that what art in this day and age is really about, just coming up with something that's so odd or so offensive or freakish that nobody's thought of it before? Isn't that the only thing that sets apart a government-subsidized crucifix in a beaker of urine from a picture of a kitten dangling from a branch under the words: "Hang on Baby, Friday's Coming"?

And while some might snicker at the kitten posters as they stroll through the west wing of the Spencer's Gifts Louvre, that is what artistic snobbery drives the masses to. The classic overcorrection of kitsch.

A few thoughts on kitsch. There is nothing cute or funny about dogs playing poker. All right? First of all, dogs cannot play poker because they don't have thumbs, and you need thumbs to shuffle and deal a deck of cards properly. And there is nothing remotely cute about animals with gambling problems. It's very sad. As a matter of fact, not one of those dogs is smiling in those pictures, because if you look closely at those paintings, then you can tell that most of them are playing with money that they can't afford to lose. And sadder still, remember it takes seven of their dollars to make one of ours.

Also, I would remind you to please take your album covers down off the wall. Album covers are for one thing and one thing only: deseeding pot.

And I have a message for the guy who took Edward Hopper's *Night Hawks* and then added Elvis behind the counter serving joe to Marilyn Monroe, Humphrey Bogart, and James Dean. Well, I just wanted you to know that I hear Tony Danza is looking for writers, okay.

And to our newly landed citizens: Well. Kick your sandals and your black socks off and make yourselves at home. That being said: Yes, I understand you are overcome by your newfound freedom. But the Statue of Liberty belongs in the New York harbor, not on your front lawn. Okay. Some of us might need to sell our homes eventually and would like to get fair market value. Okay, Olaf? Fuck the Swedes. If I'm woken up in the middle of the night one more time by yodeling, I'm gonna shove one of those Ricola horns up somebody's ass.

Listen, folks, we could go round and round and round on art, but I'm afraid I'd get sick and vomit, then somebody would put a frame around it and sell it for two grand. But I think we all agree that if we're to get back to square one on the art board, all pretense and affectation must be stripped away and we must focus on the only three immutable truths about art.

One. Art is bad if it reminds you to paint your garage.

Two. Art is really about one thing and one thing alone. Naked women. It is the one theme that transcends all time and technique. Being an artist has always been a good way for geeks to get chicks naked.

And finally, the ultimate maxim still holds true about art, "Beauty is in the eye of the head up the ass of the beholder. . . ."

Of course, that's just my opinion, I could be wrong.

Child Rearing

Now, I don't want to get off on a rant here, but raising a child today is a journey so fraught with bad directions, backseat drivers, and contradicting maps that it's a wonder we ever even make it out of the maternity hospital parking garage.

I think most (if not all) of society's ills can be traced back to poor parenting, or no parenting whatsoever. There are children in our country whose first contact with an authority figure comes while being read their Miranda rights in the backseat of a squad car.

Kids learn by example. Mommy and Daddy can say "please" and "thank you" all they want, but when their kid goes searching for role models, he's just as likely to glom on to Dennis Rodman, Bart Simpson, or some wise-ass on HBO who insists on unnecessarily ending a paragraph about being a good role model with the word "motherfucker."

You know . . . after remaining essentially unchanged for generations, the child-rearing process has undergone more bewildering mutations over the past few decades than Phyllis Diller during a long weekend on Dr. Moreau's island. The heretofore rigidly choreographed parental line-dance has morphed into a chaotic mosh pit where the Cleavers have been knocked to the floor and are being trampled to death by the Bundys. These days, the rules of parenting are more fluid than the contents of Peter O'Toole's lunch tray.

Two-parent families aren't the only game in town anymore. Single parenting has now become a viable option, because people are realizing that one caring parent is better than none—or two parents who don't give a shit.

Raising a child—alone or with a partner—may be a labor of love, but it is labor nonetheless. *It is a job.* Usually it's a fun job, but sometimes it's so frustrating, menial, and dull, it makes working the corn dog concession in the Ringworm Brothers Carnival seem like a stint in the double-O sector of Her Majesty's Secret Service. And while there's no health or dental, no vacation pay, no sick leave, no 401K, one thing you've got plenty of is job security. You need to know that you're a parent until the day you die.

Hey, take it from me. Here are some other things you need to know about parenting:

Children think farts are hysterically funny. And you know why? Because farts are hysterically funny.

Children were designed to disassemble anything. Given enough time and Lick-Em-Ade Sticks, a seven-year-old could break into Bill Clinton's burger vault and convince the Secret Service that his imaginary friend Mr. Noodles made him do it. There are primal forces of nature at work in children.

Okay. Remember on Sunday mornings you used to sleep in, drink a cup of coffee in bed, read the paper, turn on some Sinatra music, maybe make love. All right, that . . . is over. God might have rested on the seventh day, but only because he sent his son to live with another family. From here on in, you wake up on Sunday morning to a sticky kid who crawled into bed with you, had a dream about Splash Mountain, and whizzed all over your sheets. Okay? That's Sunday morning.

You know, if you have a son, he is going to hit you in the balls at least once or twice a year, if you're lucky. They claim it's an accident. I don't think so. There are piñatas that get hit less than my balls.

Folks, I don't want to lay it all out for you, because then you'd miss the ride. Everybody's got their own opinion on how you can be a good parent. I don't want to bore you with the intricacies of mine. One thing I would tell you, though, is be there for them.

That's the main requirement of parenting. Just be there. Think of yourself as Chance the Gardener with Baby Wipes. You don't always have to be brilliant, you don't always have to be charming, you don't always have to be the best. You just have to be theirs, unequivocally.

I'm telling you to take parenting seriously. That means that when you give Mr. Sperm a laminated all-access backstage pass to Miss Egg or vice versa, you do so with the knowledge that if you bring a life into this world, that life is *your responsibility*. Even if it means missing the prom, or driving an econo-van instead of a Viper, or being thrown up on more frequently than Fifth Avenue on St. Patrick's Day.

And finally . . . if everything I've said up to this point hasn't made you realize how serious a commitment having a child is, maybe this will: Baby Nikes are 85 bucks a pair.

Of course, that's just my opinion, I could be wrong.

White People

White people will pay to see anything. It's amazing. I mean, really. I'm asking you. What's up with whitey?

Now, I don't want to get off on a rant here, but what is there to say about a race whose only significant contributions to our culture in the past half century have been Jell-O shots, referring to Wednesday as "Humpday," and the cosmic nightmare that was Vanilla Ice? And on behalf of all white people, I'd just like to say: We're sorry about Vanilla Ice. We didn't know he was going to do that. He didn't mention it at any of the meetings.

You know, we've been in the driver's seat so long that we're starting to nod off at the wheel. Let's face it—we're a bunch of goofy motherfuckers. White people have occasionally come up with a beneficial tidbit for mankind, but more often than not we've trashed this place like John Bonham and Keith Moon fighting over the last bottle of Glenlivet in the minibar at the room in the Château Marmont.

I am a white guy, I don't deny that. In fact, I'm pretty up front about it. When the tollbooth guy tells me to have a nice day, I say "okeydokey." On my home stereo the treble is turned up higher than the bass. And when the frozen yogurt costs four dollars and twenty-six cents, I give them a five and then I say "Wait, I think I have a penny."

I mean, what cool stuff can white people really claim as their own? Rock and roll? Stolen from the bluesmen of the Mississippi delta. Smoking? The Indians. Railroads? Built by the Chinese. When you think about it, white people always just let others do all the work, then we step in and try and take the credit. We are the cultural Larry Tate.

We elect Bob Dornan clones to do our immigration bidding under the guise of a free country. But mostly, I'll be honest, we are scared of not being on top anymore.

White people aren't having as much fun because we're too busy just trying to hang on to what we've got. We are obsessed with the idea that we have to get ahead and succeed, we have to look like the white people in the ads, our muffins have to be as fluffy and moist as Martha Stewart's, we have to remember to tape *Friends* lest we be left in the dust at the watercooler on Friday morning, and our lawns have to have more of an edge than Gary Old-man after drinking a pot of espresso and realizing he's out of cigarettes. I mean, just ask Michael Jackson, he'll tell you things were less complicated and more fun back when he was a minority.

And what do we do with those among us who are the whitest of the white? Why, we make them our kings. Look at our last couple of Presidents. Bush? Christ, Bush is beyond white. . . . Bush is fucking transparent, all right. Next to George Bush, I am Hammer.

And Bill Clinton is the über–White Guy; we ought to just change the national anthem to "Whiter Shade of Pale." I mean, Clinton is an aw-shucks white boy who loves fast food and gals with big hair. He's the next-door neighbor who flirts with your wife while he sweet-talks you into lending him your brand-new band saw which he never intends to give back.

So what can we start doing to get some respect back to our people from the other cultures? I'd like to offer the following suggestions to my pigmentally challenged brethren.

Number one. *Star Wars* is a great movie. But when married couples show up dressed in full Luke Skywalker and Princess Leia regalia, the force won't stop other people from taking your laser sword and sticking it up your ass.

Two. Cheez Whiz is not something you eat. It is something you consult a urologist for.

Three. When you meet African Americans, don't laugh nervously at everything they say. Believe it or not, all black people are not Richard Pryor. Some of them have horrible senses of humor and are just making normal conversation with you.

Number four. Dinner theater. Only Whitey could have thought, "I liked *West Side Story*. But you know what was missing? Pork chops."

Five. When I see tractor pulls advertised on television, I want to douse my skin in baby oil and sit in front of a sun lamp for sixteen straight hours. Okay?

Number six. Kathie Lee Gifford . . . you mustn't ever sing again.

Seven. Ken Burns—stop. I know your heart is in the right place, but life is too short to sit through Jason fucking Robards reading another four-hour letter General Custer wrote to his goddamned wife from the Battle of Little Big Snore. All right. Somebody tell Ken Burns that a documentary on the Civil War doesn't have to last a year longer than the actual war.

Number eight. It's not spray-on hair. It's *paint*. When you use it, you are painting your head. So, if you're going to paint your head, then while you're at it, why don't you just wood-panel your cock, okay?

Number nine. If you ever meet Nelson Mandela, don't call him "Bro."

And finally, don't call the guys from your bowling team "your homeys." Don't try and get your fiddle band on

Dennis Miller

Showtime at the Apollo. Don't try and break-dance at your own wedding. And all white people, everywhere: Stop rapping, okay? You aren't Snoop Doggy Dog. You're not even Deputy Dog. You're white. So act white. Peace. Out.

Of course, that's just my opinion, I could be wrong.

UFOs

Why are Americans so reluctant to welcome anybody from Mexico and so enamored—witness the grosses for *Independence Day*—of the idea of encountering creatures from another planet?

Now, I don't want to get off on a rant here, but it seems like nowadays you can't throw a rock without hitting somebody who'll claim it was a UFO.

As life on this planet swirls at an ever-increasing speed down the crapper, is it any wonder that we're becoming more and more fixated with this notion of life elsewhere?

It all began in the fifties when we saw an astronomical increase in the number of UFO sightings. In fact, before 1947 there were next to no reports of UFOs. Is it just a coincidence that everyone began to see flying saucers about the same time everyone began seeing Communists? World War II was over and we needed something new to fear.

In 1947 something crashed in Roswell, New Mexico. Some believe four aliens were discovered at the site and that their remains, as well as the flying saucer, are being held in an air force installation a hundred miles north of Las Vegas known as Area 51. UFO-olgists insist that the four aliens, and manager Brian Epstein, accidentally crashed their own flying saucer. Yeah, because they can travel 350 million light-years dodging black holes, asteroids, and comets, but those New Mexico telephone wires are a real bitch. Hey, I think two of the four aliens might have survived the wreck, escaped from Area 51, and made it to Vegas, where they've been doing nine shows a week under the names Siegfried and Roy!

Now, true "believers" say that Area 51 is definitely hiding something, because if you go there, they won't let you in and they won't tell you what they have there. You know why that is? Because it's a fucking military installation! All right, what do you think if you go to Areas 1 through 50 you're going to get some chardonnay and a piece of Gouda? No, you're not. You're going to get turned away faster than Roger Clinton trying to get backstage at a Marilyn Manson concert.

Now, some believe that there is an authentic film of an autopsy on one of the Roswell aliens. I saw the film on Fox, I believe it was sandwiched between a very special

Martin and a very special *Party of Five* and I thought the autopsy was as authentic as a piece of total bullshit can be. By the way, you know what the autopsy found? Traces of O.J.'s blood.

In addition to the Area 51 freaks, there are those who legitimize the existence of aliens vis-à-vis the appearance of crop patterns that resemble the symbol that Prince uses as his name etched into an okra field outside Mt. Pilot. All right, occasionally bizarre patterns can be seen if you and Mike the Crop Duster who dated Bea Benaderet's lesbian daughter Bobbi Jo fly over the fields out back of the Shady Rest. Some say it's a landing marker for aliens. I say it's Uncle Joe with an IV drip of grain alcohol and a weed whacker.

Another core ingredient of UFO studies is the abduction by aliens. Under hypnosis, the abductees' recollections all share the same characteristics: long stretches of time unaccounted for, strange bruises on the body, a suspicion of sexual violation . . . is it just me, or does alien abduction sound amazingly like spring break?

Listen, it's a natural tendency to look skyward for the next shiny thing to answer our prayers. That's why people flock to UFO conventions in the hope that when the inevitable mass landing does happen, the star gods will first want to get in touch with the mentally unstable among us.

The purest defining event of the UFO culture has got to be the *Star Trek* convention. Not since the pope and Cardinal O'Connor spoke to a symposium of nuns catered by the Amish has so little sexual experience been assembled in one room.

Dennis Miller

Hey, look, I would be the first one to tell you I would welcome aliens, because I am running out of people to despise on this planet.

Despite the barnacles of cynicism that resolutely encrust my hull, I do believe that there is life other than ours somewhere other than Earth. I just don't think they're coming here. I don't know who they are or what they drive, but I assume that they, like I, stick to the tenet that the less you have to do with your neighbors, the better off it is for everyone involved.

To an extraterrestrial, planet Earth, at best, would be like the Vince Lombardi rest stop along the Jersey Turnpike. Chances are they stopped off here once to try and stretch their tiny gray limbs, pick up a nut log, and take a leak out of one of their forty-seven penises.

But on the off chance that there are any super-advanced alien beings out there, first of all, thanks for buying the book. And now I want you to listen up, Kaldar of Romula Five. When you do come here and abduct one of us, invariably, might I add, one of us from a rural address, please stay out of our asses. Okay?

There's nothing in our asses that will help you and your dying planet. Life . . . life . . . I thank you. My asshole thanks you. Life is tough enough out there in grow country without you proctonauts downing a couple of cases of Zima and getting your moon rocks off checking on Jethro's oil.

Of course, that's just my opinion, I could be wrong.

The Afterlife

Eventually, we all have to leave the building, don't we? It's just—what's out there, Uhura?

Now, I don't want to get off on a rant here, but as more and more aging baby boomers peer through their bifocals at the haggard Lance Henriksen face of their own mortality, one question seems to occur with numbing frequency: Where do we go after last call at Bistro Earth?

As a forty-three-year-old man, I am starting to ponder concepts like my own endgame, not so much in a Dionne Warwick way, but as a means with which to acclimate myself to facing the inevitable. I know people say "Life begins at forty." Yeah, if you're the fucking

Highlander, but, you know, the rest of us are trying to make sense out of the indecipherable babble of everyone else's best guess as to what awaits us behind door Number 3 in Monty's Death Jar.

Do we go on a journey into something more magnificent or do we merely get buried and remade into bridge mix for worms? Well, you know, we just don't know. And that question often tugs on us harder than Newt Gingrich trying to water-ski.

Death haunts us because the only guarantee that comes with the gift of life is that sooner or later you're going to have to return that gift to whatever cosmic Nordstrom we inhabit. The afterlife is a subject that's inspired more speculation than how Melissa Etheridge's girlfriend got pregnant.

You know, I would like to believe that when I get to the Pearly Gates I will be greeted by St. Peter, and he'll say that he's a big fan of the show and I don't have to queue up with the rest of the dead losers and then a big doorman with a headset halo and black leather wings unhitches the velvet rope and waves me in. That's what I'd like to believe. . . .

But for all I know, St. Pete is just another pissed-off DMV zombie who makes you go to the end of the stooge line behind the guy who had one tai chi lesson and went into a biker bar to test it out . . . he's standing in front of you there in the crane position, with a pool cue sticking out of his ass. . . . Blunt side in.

Then the next thing in the eternal life is you get to review all the moments of your life. That's great—having to watch dailies of all the stuff you'd rather forget from your earlier days. Scenes like the time you figured out how to fuck your toy cement mixer when you were twelve. How about the time you ate a Castaneda-sized portion of buttons at a college party and thought your roommate was a giant suck-locust so you ran nude through a mall with a Doors 45 stuck on your penis to warn the villagers.

So while we can all pretty much agree on what heaven must be like, hell, like Winston Smith's rat cage, is a subjective thing. It's what you find most loathsome and frightening in your heart of hearts, and it is forever. It's sitting in the *Clockwork Orange* chair through an ever-repeating double feature of *Showgirls* and *Stop! or My Mom Will Shoot*. It's being stuck in a never-ending traffic jam in mid-August with no air-conditioning and a radio that gets only the All Rosie Perez, All the Time station.

Philosopher Jean-Paul Sartre once said, "Hell is other people." And he should know, because he lived in France. About the only evidence we have to go on as far as the afterlife is concerned is the testimony of people who have had near death experiences. And they all describe the same phenomenon. Rushing at breakneck speed through a long, dark tunnel toward a bright light at the end. Hey, you call it a near death experience, I call it riding on Amtrak, okay. Potato, potahto, derailo, derallo.

But near death isn't enough, is it? What we really need to do is to talk to somebody with a cellular on the other side who's got metaphysical roam.

Now, when I was a kid, we got a ouija board and we proceeded to convince ourselves that we had discovered a direct connection to the world of the unseen. I realized

Dennis Miller

that maybe it wasn't that precise a device when we lost the sliding thing and replaced it with a Cool Whip lid with a thumbtack in it. I was getting suspicious anyway when I noticed that all of the spirits we contacted misspelled the exact same words that my brother did.

Now, the latter-day ouija board is the channelers, and channelers, for a hefty fee, will sit you down at a table, back-light a crystal, turn on some *Tesh at Red Rocks* bootleg tape, and then pop in and out of characters so paper thin, they couldn't get past the table read at *Renegade*. And this stuff is rife in L.A. I would remind you, though, that most people in Hollywood barely have one person inside of them, let alone two hundred.

Simply put, if there were no money to be made from summoning the dead, channeling would be about as popular as Marla Maples at a benefit screening of *The First Wives Club*. Okay.

So if much of man's dabblings in the afterlife distill down into nonsense, why does it hold so much fascination for us? And for the answer to that question, we must go to the afterlife's P.R. firm, Organized Religion. Promising us eternal bliss and threatening us with hell and damnation are the bullwhip and chair that keep us from trying to maul our trainer.

Well, it's ironic that an argument about finality could go on and on, but that about sums it up. So let's just leave it at this. Your big three brand-name creeds all agree on one thing. Sammy Hagar was a mistake.

Of course, that's just my opinion, I could be wrong.

Gun Control

Now, I don't want to get off on a rant here, but I think it's time we called a cease-fire in the debate over gun control.

The police have powerful weapons and the criminals have powerful weapons and you and I are left with eight dead bolts, a nine-hundred-dollar-a-month cable bill, and we've been reduced to asking the pizza boy as he slips the Big Foot under the door, "Hey, have the leaves turned out there yet?"

Americans are more armed than the octopus at the Chernobyl aquarium. And yet you talk gun control with anyone from the NRA and they go to the Constitution faster than *SNL* cast members go to their cue cards.

Listen, the men who wrote the Constitution meant it as a guideline for the law. Much like when Martha Stewart bakes botanically correct Concord grape leaves for the top of her pie crusts. You can't really go by what she says. Don't you see? You'll end up like her. Yeah, the founding fathers said we had a right to bear arms. They also said we had a right to *own other human beings.* Now, thankfully, we've moved on from that soupçon of divine enlightenment, and it's about time we start taking the Wite-Out to other parts of the Constitution.

I mean, come on, it's over two hundred years old and we don't usually pay attention to anything that ancient. If we did, American life could be summed up in three words: "President Bob Dole." You know, when the Constitution was written, guns were an essential tool for survival.

Now, granted, several of our Founding Fathers were probably in the dementia stage of syphillis at that constitutional rewrite session, but surely they didn't mean that this right to bear arms takes precedence over living in an orderly and safe society.

We needed an armed, well-regulated militia at the time of our country's breach-of-contract birth because we just stole it from the Brits and there was a good chance that the little bald guy from Benny Hill and a whole shitload of snaggletoothed redcoats were coming over the hill any day on the H.M.S. *Richard Branson* to get it back. But nowadays a citizen militia has become about as necessary as bodyguards for Peter Frampton.

You know, guns are part of this country's DNA, they're inextricably woven into the fiber of our psyche. America was founded by rebels, liberated by guerrillas, and settled in no small part by outlaws.

Now, piggyback onto that lineage an unhealthy Bob Dornan-like mistrust of the unfamiliar, fold in a heaping helping of Paranoia Helper, and you conclude, my friends, that this country is overflowing with enough leavening agents to create an uprising that is going to make Mount St. Helens seem like Vendela fake-smoking a Cohiba on the cover of *Cigar Aficionado*.

Now, obviously we can't ban all guns, because many of them are used for the recreational sport of hunting. And people have to hunt because it's a simple fact that deer have to die. They have to be taken out, because if they aren't, they're just going to keep dashing through the forest, frolicking in the fields, and nibbling the leaves and berries off trees and bushes. I mean, come on, Bambi is begging for it. The deer might as well just refuse to sell their casino to the Corleone family.

So, what are the solutions?

One recent plan is the guns for toys or guns for concert tickets exchanges. Recently I saw a promotion where for each gun you handed in you got two tickets to an L.A. Clippers game. Now, that doesn't work out too well, because after watching the Clippers you want to kill yourself and you don't have a gun. It is literally an O. Henry story waiting to be written.

New York City tried information, installing the nation's first "death clock" in Times Square. This large, lighted sign would count handgun deaths in the country, like a McDonald's sign counts hamburger sales. It didn't work because there were people in Times Square who would shoot you just to watch the damn sign change. Then they'd ask a cop to initial their score.

Okay, so information isn't working, giveaways aren't working, and we all agree it's fantasyland to believe that we can get rid of all the guns. But I think that any right-minded individual would agree that we should make guns harder to get than an eight o'clock table at Morton's on Monday night.

And what are the specifics of making it harder? Well, first off, let's light a fire under the pale, pasty, white, cellulite-ridden asses of those asses down in Washington, D.C. You want gun control? Get rid of the metal detectors around the Capitol building. Take away the Secret Service protection for all politicians. Christ, by next week the worst thing you'll have to worry about is drive-by *shoutings*, which, I might add, are protected by the First Amendment.

And that's fine with me, 'cause without freedom of speech, well, I'm just the white guy running the malt shop on *Moesha*.

Of course, that's just my opinion, I could be wrong.

The Fall
of the
Middle Class

Now, I don't want to get off on a rant here, but the chasm between the haves and the have-nots in this country is beginning to make the Grand Canyon look like the space between Japanese rail commuters. The socioeconomic disparity between the classes in America is yawning like George Sanders watching a fishing show hosted by fed chairman Alan Greenspan.

From birth, America was the bold new experiment. Idealism made reality in the soft clay of a burgeoning democracy. This grand nation of dreams now has the look of the worn, tired diner waitress who's seen way too much.

A shrinking portion of the population controls a growing portion of the money, and more and more of the middle class are finding themselves stuck on the high-prices-low-wages hamster wheel.

Being middle class in America today is like being George Jetson walking Astro on that treadmill. No one knows how to stop this crazy thing. I know that some of you are probably launching into that reflexive "greatest-country - in - the - world - land - of - unfettered - economic - opportunity" Irving Berlin song-and-dance number right now, but there are some very nice, hardworking people out there who *just aren't making it*. And they're not all teenage single high-school-dropout crackhead moms either. Regular people in unexotic circumstances are finding themselves unable to afford to own a home or send their kids to college. Dual-income families are often living a paycheck away from setting up house in the nearest Starbucks doorway. In 1990s America, you're either driving the Rolls or you're washing its windshield for spare change.

How is it that a country that hails democracy and capitalism as the only fair and just system of empowering the people has ended up more top-heavy than Anna Nicole Smith in a centrifuge?

What people lack these days is a way out of the class they started in. Short of being able to decide who your parents are, how can someone of limited means make a better life for themselves these days? People no longer work like dogs to get ahead, they work like dogs just to stay where they are and not become homeless. Take a look at what the average American has been earning during the past twenty years and you'd see more growth on

Doogie Howser's face. Once you're down, trying to get back up is like shoveling while it's snowing. Either you're rich or you're poor. The situation is becoming as bipolar as the day room at Bellevue.

And what kind of toll does this steady yet dyspeptic diet of economic extremes take on us and our children? Well, all of us have become more frightened than Lance Loud being introduced to the fans at a Ted Nugent concert.

Look, I'm for capitalism. All the other systems have worked out about as well as a Lee Greenwood booking in Baghdad. But we need to start holding government, the big teat, tittie el grande, mammary avec collosso, capo di titti immensia . . . boobus gigandus, titasaurus rex, the *Hindenboob,* oh, the humammary, anyway, government, we need to start holding it, did I mention the sweater meat mountains, and the brave sherpas who died on the north face of their aureola glacier fields, well, like I was saying, we need to start holding government accountable for the equitable distribution of the tax money they harvest.

I think the classic American equation dictates that a man should be able to keep one dollar for every one he gives away. We have to make sure that those carrion birds up on Capitol Hill get the money into the right beaks as efficiently as possible rather than siphoning it off to pay for their state-sponsored junkets to Paris to buy their wives a new set of diamond-studded ben-wa balls.

I know it's fashionable right now to take the approach that it's better to cut someone's leg off than it is to give them a leg up. Well, I know enough about history to know

Dennis Miller

that we can do this the easy way or we can all do it the hard way. The easy way is everybody should pay their fair share so we have better schools and social programs to help decent people who don't have it so good. The hard way is people keep being selfish and greedy and insisting on preferential treatment.

And sure as the turned-up nose on their face, they'll eventually get preferential treatment by being allowed to preboard the cart that takes them to the guillotine.

Me, I have a nice home, I provide for my family and try to make them comfortable, but I'm not a pig about it. I mean, just the other day I was lounging around my Olympic-sized pool shaped like a middle finger and filled with Evian water and I was commanding my personal toast chef, Armando, to burn hundred-dollar bills just for shits and giggles, and all of a sudden I realized that the third-world orphan I pay to walk my solid gold dog is late, but do I have him killed? No, I don't.

I merely have the guy I hire to lick all my cars clean break his knees with one of my platinum-shafted polo mallets, taking pains to ensure that he doesn't bleed all over my mink lawn.

You know why? Because all of this hasn't gone to my head.

Of course, that's just my opinion, I could be wrong.

Friends

According to new medical research, being around friends boosts the immune system. Unless, of course, you're sharing needles with them.

Now, I don't want to get off on a rant here, but with cable and satellite TV and the recent dizzying advances in telecommunications making it possible for almost anyone to maintain a state of continuous Major Tom–like solitude, friends have never been considered less necessary, or been more important, than they are right now.

As technology encases us in an ever-tighter chrysalis devoid of the most basic interpersonal contact, many

Americans find themselves on a frantic, Tailgunner Joe McCarthy–like hunt for comrades that can leave you feeling lonelier than Marvin Hamlisch at Lollapalooza.

Now, as you might have guessed, I make friends as easily as the Swiss Family Robinson made ice.

But I was better when I was a kid. When we are young, friends give us the confidence in ourselves to do things we would never do without their influence. Whether it's going out for a team, asking a girl for a date, or hot-wiring our mom's car so that we could make a beer run to the L'il General Convenience Mart but it was closed so we found a brick and smashed the window and stole a couple of cases and got chased by the cops but the "friend" took off in our mom's car, leaving us to take the fall for the . . . Mikey, you little shithead!

Because we are so desperate for companionship, we often mistakenly believe people are our friends when they're not. Like my postman. Every day he comes to my house and gives me exciting letters, stimulating magazines, and shiny presents. You know, fun stuff, and I'm always glad to see him. So usually I don't leave the house until he comes by, because, you know, I want to see what he's got for me today. And I figure since he is always whistling and smiling, well, you know, he's glad to see me too. So one day I offer him a glass of juice. He takes it, and I'm thinking, hey, I have a new friend. But then the next day, when I invite him in to watch the showcase round on *The Price Is Right,* he says he's too busy. He says he has other rounds to make. And, you know, at first it felt like someone had ripped my chest right open and hacked my heart into little pieces. I tried not to let him see me cry. But then my wife sat down next to me on the curb and explained that he isn't really my friend. That these aren't gifts from him but things that other people have mailed to me.

You see, he's just delivering these things because that's his job, he's a postman. And when he smiles or waves at me, that's because he likes his job. Not because he wants me to be his friend.

And despite what you've been told, your dog is not your best friend. Oh, he'll act like your best friend, especially when he's hungry or when you've got the clicker and he wants to watch *The Bone Ranger* on Spice Channel. Oh, yeah, he'll have you buying into that man's-best-friend horseshit until it's three o'clock in the morning and you need someone to pick you up from a party, and then suddenly man's best friend is screening his calls. Dukey, you're a little motherfucker, all right?

But when you're truly in the company of good friends, you're more comfy than Ed Begley Jr. in an electric car on his way to the recycling center with a trunk full of empties and a solar-powered auto-suck.

And if you have trouble making friends, now you can meet people on the Internet. This is great. You think you are talking to a cute, recently divorced blond coed, when in reality you are pouring out your sexual needs to a fifty-year-old cross-country truck driver named Skeeter who's wearing a camisole and panty hose.

I think the very best way to tell if you can be friends with someone is whether or not you can make each other laugh. I've got a friend who made me laugh so hard one day last week, milk actually came out of my nose. And I haven't had any milk in over two years.

But no matter how strong your relationship is, eventually you'll encounter the biggest hurdle a friendship can ever possibly face. Someday, no matter how much you pray it won't happen, no matter how much you do everything in your power to prevent it, no matter how much you fight it with every fiber of your being, eventually your friend is going to be successful.

Hey, you all know what a friend is. A friend is someone who can watch twelve straight hours of the Cartoon Network Jonny-Quest-a-Thon without uttering one word then get up and leave and not even say good-bye to me.

A friend is someone with whom I can go to a restaurant and spend the entire meal on the cell phone talking to my agent.

A friend is someone with whom I can lock the automatic car windows, let loose with a taco grande carpet bomb fart, and still get a high-five off him.

And, finally, to me, a *best* friend is someone who can keep a secret, someone who likes sports, someone who'll let me store some of my personal effects at his place, no questions asked, someone who doesn't judge my mood swings, no matter how extreme they get, and most important, someone who will drive me around in a white Bronco as I hold a gun to my head.

Of course, that's just my opinion, I could be wrong.

Cops

Boy, I don't envy cops. A cop is a person who leaves every day for work and doesn't know if they'll ever make it home alive. In other words, they're just like any other person trying to earn a living in L.A.

Now, I don't want to get off on a rant here, but the glamorous and exciting image of cops we have from TV shows and movies gives you as accurate a picture of reality as watching a Bill Clinton press conference dubbed in Swahili while you're high on amyl nitrite poppers. Or, for that matter, a Clinton press conference under any circumstances.

Now, before I criticize how other people do their jobs, I always ask myself, "Could I do it?" And the answer here is no, because the job of cop can be more foul than George Kennedy without his BreathAsure. Hey, I just don't have the temperament. The first time some Chiclet-brain I pulled over for a traffic ticket gave me that "Hey, I pay your salary" rap, I'd be too tempted to flip him a quarter and say, "Here's a refund, fuckwad," and then I'd drag his ass out of the car and start beating on him like he was a Hitler piñata at a Mossad picnic. Yeah, if I were a cop, I'd go through stun guns like Bing Crosby after noticing his kids weren't playing with their new toys on Christmas morning.

Cops day to day have to deal with more violence than Tina Turner did when Ike lost the Grammy. And they have to deal with the same violent criminals over and over again. The greased pneumatic tube that we laughingly refer to as our legal system has criminals back on the streets before the arresting officer can finish the K-2–sized mound of paperwork on their original arrest. It's frustrating for the cops. It's like when I make jokes about Newt Gingrich being a big fat asshole. Just when I think I'm done with him, he becomes an even bigger, fatter ass crater and I have to do even more jokes about him.

By the way, did you know that cops in England don't even carry guns? All they have are those wooden sticks. And do you know how difficult it is to toss a bullet up in the air and then use a stick to smack it into a criminal? Pretty difficult.

But back to the good old U.S. of AK-47. And how about a mention for the most unheralded cop of all—the police dog. Super group of selfless little pooches, there. Working long hours all day looking for drugs and not even getting a chance to sniff a nice butt, and when they go home to the doghouse, they're under too much stress and strain to even be able to eat their kibbles or mount their bitch. Thank you, dog cop.

This is not to say there aren't some bad two-legged cops out there. For instance, when the police kick open the door and catch you and your wife fixing the camshaft in the methamphetamine lab, why do they always scream, "Freeze, motherfuckers!" Hey, a simple "freeze" will do, guttermouth. My wife is in the room and the kids are sleeping in the back. Show a little respect for the family unit, please.

But these are quibbles. Ninety-nine percent of the time, my allegiances lie with the men and women in blue. The rights of the criminals should never supersede the rights of good, decent, hardworking people. As far as I'm concerned, the rights of the criminal begin and end the moment a criminal is caught in the act.

Sometimes I yearn for the simpler days, when cops didn't have to be so politically correct and touchy-feely and compassionate. Like Kojak. He was just a crazy, bald son of a bitch who didn't give a shit. Like when this couple from the Midwest whose daughter moves to New York and becomes a prostitute gets murdered, and they're in the station house sobbing and Kojak walks in and says: "Yeah, yeah, yeah, she was Mom's apple pie, the Fourth of July . . . SHE WAS A HOOKER!" Telly, we hardly knew ye.

Now we've gone to the other end of the spectrum, where the police have to drive alongside the armed fugitive, placing themselves and innocent civilians in harm's way until PCP boy runs out of psycho gas. It's true. One phenomenon currently taking place in the city of Los Angeles is the fully televised high-speed prime-time chase that all the local television stations insist on carrying in its entirety. Hey, Airwolf, blow the fucking tires out and put *Frasier* back on, okay?

Sure, I think cops can be brutal sometimes, because it is a brutal world we live and make them work in. But while we are sleeping in our homes, they are out on the dirty boulevard trying to make it safe for us in the morning. And for all you ACLU members out there without an A-C-L-U-E: When you hear a noise outside your house in the middle of the night and you fear for your life and call 911, just be glad it's cops who show up at your front door and not Alan Dershowitz, because, believe me, if it was Dershowitz, you'd end up more fucked than a tour group in Amsterdam led by Wilt Chamberlain on Spanish fly.

Of course, that's just my opinion, I could be wrong.